Humor   7.50

The Lore of Averages

Printed and bound in Great Britain by MPG Books Ltd, Bodmin

Arcane is an imprint of Sanctuary Publishing Limited
Sanctuary House, 45–53 Sinclair Road
London W14 0NS, United Kingdom

www.sanctuarypublishing.com

ISBN: 1-86074-617-9

The Lore of Averages

Facts, Figures And Stories That Make
Everyday Life Extraordinary

Karen Farrington

arcane

– ASK THE AUDIENCE –

In case you were wondering whether averages reveal anything other than the mediocre, rest assured. They do. For some curious reason, humankind seems to be better at solving certain types of problems collectively rather than relying on individual experts. Say what you like about the man or woman in the street, but the mean (ie average) viewpoint is very often the right one.

A good example is cited by James Surowiecki in his book *The Wisdom Of Crowds*. In 1906 a British scientist from Plymouth, Francis Galton, was attending a country fair at which people were being challenged to guess the weight of an ox after it had been slaughtered and dressed. Eight hundred people had a go, many of them butchers and farmers, but also hundreds who had no specialist knowledge.

Galton (clearly bored by the other stands) added up all the guessed weights and divided by the number of entrants. In other words, if all the entrants had voted, this average figure would have been their chosen entry. Galton expected it to be hopelessly wrong. He reckoned most people were poorly educated and ill-informed and that society could only operate successfully in the hands of the intelligentsia. Imagine his surprise then when the result was announced. The slaughtered ox weighed 543.3 kg (1,198 lb). The crowd had collectively guessed at 542.8 kg (1,197 lb).

This isn't coincidence at work. It's the reason why, if you're on *Who Wants To Be A Millionaire*, you're better off asking the audience to help rather than phoning a clever friend. Friends get the answer right 65 per cent of the time; audiences produce a near-perfect return of 91 per cent. But be warned. Surowiecki points out that for the trick to work, groups should be diverse, they need to make decisions relatively independently and they musn't all be getting information from the same sources. If you want to check this, ask anyone who lost money buying shares in the 1990s' dot.com boom.

– HIGH ROLLERS –

On average, people going fishing are ten times more likely to be injured than those going to an amusement park.

In America there are 450 amusement parks with 606 roller-coasters. Out of 320 million visitors in 2002, there were 6,500 reported injuries (including sunburn) and one fatality.

Those are the figures the amusement park people like to quote, anyway, adding that more than nine times as many accidents were caused by bicycles and basketball in 2001. Fears still abound about the bodily effects of thrilling modern rides like the 'Accelerator', which travels from 0 to 130 kph (0–80 mph) in two seconds.

Such concerns don't enter the heads of roller-coaster riding children who love the climbing and dramatic dipping of the rides. And some children never grow up, maintaining a Peter Pan passion for fairground trips into adulthood and even into old age. For them exists The Roller Coaster Club of Great Britain, a group for like-minded individuals hooked on the exhilaration of roller-coaster rides. According to its website, it has more than 1,200 members from 15 different countries, each the veteran of 100 different roller-coaster rides. When RCCGB members visit an amusement park, they are likely to stay for eight hours and will park themselves on the big rides 40 times.

The group began in 1988 and now organises regular trips to parks in Britain and Europe. There are also a biannual visits to the USA, in which two coach-loads of members ride between 80 and 100 roller-coasters in 16 days.

It was in America that some members experienced the ultimate in white-knuckle riding. An operator in one park agreed to turn off the brakes on the carriages of a ride called 'Wild Thing'. The name probably tells you all you need to know about the experience that awaited the brave participants. One RCCGB member Colin Anderson takes up the story: 'The park had never done it before and a lot of the workers there came on the ride with us. Instead of braking before you get to the top, we just went full speed all the way round.' Did I mention that one qualification for club membership was the ownership of iron guts?

– HOLIDAY NIGHTMARES –

Four out of ten children prefer television to the beach.

The lures of building sandcastles, rock pooling and splashing in the shallows are no longer sufficient to entice children to the beach, a survey has discovered.

When Thomson Holidays conducted a poll among 2,095 people, the company discovered that 42 per cent of children preferred watching TV to beaching it up, while 26 per cent admitted they would choose Gameboy games above beach games if they could. One in five like sending text messages better than sun, sea and surf. Overall, just 50 per cent of those questioned said they were ready to sample new adventure sports like water skiing while they were on holiday. Definitely big sitters, rather than big hitters, in the making.

– PHONE HOME –

A survey among 1,000 adults conducted in 2002 discovered that one in 20 people used their mobile phone on the doorstep to tell their partners they were home.

– COKE BLIZZARD –

Drug-sniffing dogs typically take six minutes to check a car – and they rarely make mistakes.

Geography has been kind to the cocaine gangsters of Central America. To the south, farmers in Bolivia and Peru provide a steady flow of unrefined cocaine. All the cartels need do is cut in some chemicals, add a healthy mark-up and head for the US–Mexico border.

Of the 86,700 kg (190,000 lb) of cocaine seized in the USA during the 2001 fiscal year, 40,000 kg (88,000 lb) was shipped in via Mexico. The 3,218-km (2,000-mile) long frontier is a largely unpatrolled, unfenced, unpopulated desert, and although the government has a few strategically placed radar balloons and a handful of surveillance planes, it's not much of a deterrent.

On the upside, there aren't many tarmac roads. As a result, many coke smugglers still try to sneak in through the world's busiest land border post – San Ysidro, south of San Diego – where 80 pedestrians and car passengers pass through immigration every minute of every day.

Customs officers use some serious hi-tech wizardry to wheedle out the drug couriers from this heaving mass of humanity. Gadgets include density-busters (a type of ultrasound scanner), X-ray machines and digital cameras capable of processing 40,000 car registration plates a day. But technology isn't everything.

In 1997 a Chevrolet estate car imported from Mexico to Germany was impounded in Hamburg after X-rays showed it contained 54 kg (118 lb) of cocaine. Six years later the vehicle was auctioned off and the new owner promptly discovered 11 bags of a funny white powder in the boot. Back in '97 this would have had a street value in

Germany of 500,000 euros (£350,000). Customs officials said the 1997 software used to scan the car had not been sophisticated enough.

Certainly not as sophisticated as a sniffer dog. A German shepherd – one of several breeds used by US Customs – has 220 million sensory cells in its nose, 44 times more than the average human. These animals typically take six minutes to check a car and they rarely make mistakes. One trafficker tried vacuum-sealing his coke stash before smearing it in grease, sealing it again, and suspending the whole caboodle inside his car petrol tank.

Didn't fool the dog.

– TOAST TO SCIENCE –

Sod's Law clearly states that if a piece of toast falls on the floor, it always goes butter side down. However, according to research by Robert Matthews of Aston University, Birmingham, the actual figure for butter-side landings is more like 62 per cent. He reached this conclusion by persuading more than 1,000 children to drop a total of 9,821 slices. The butter hit the dirt on 6,101 occasions. 'There's a more serious side to my work,' Matthews mused later. 'I just can't remember what it is.'

– USELESS THIEF –

Just over 6,500 vehicles a week are stolen in Britain – an annual average of 1.6 offences per 1,000 people.

Some thieves use force, some are crafty and some are lucky. A few, though, are just plain useless. Included in the latter category is the case of a 21-year-old man who in June 2004 pleaded guilty to the attempted theft of a car parked in the

Devon village of Kingskerswell. Torbay magistrates heard how he'd been thrown out of a nearby guest house after a binge drinking session and decided to steal the car from a driveway to visit a friend.

Describing his efforts as 'the most pathetic case of trying to steal a vehicle I've come across in a very long time', prosecutor James Bax said the man released the handbrake and opened the driver's side door to get a better view. The car rolled forward, the door was forced against a pillar, the thief's head got trapped in the door and the car owner heard his screams. The man was eventually released by sniggering cops. He got four months in jail.

– SOCCER BANKERS –

The average crowd in the English Premiership during 2003/04 was 34,884 strong.

Premiership football clubs in England have never had it so good. Average home crowd attendances at the six best-supported clubs in 2003/04 were 67,640 (Manchester United), 51,966 (Newcastle), 46,834 (Manchester City), 42,677 (Liverpool), 41,234 (Chelsea) and 38,837 (Everton).

So spare a thought for those at the other end of the football spectrum, particularly East Stirlingshire `FC of the Scottish Third Division. During the 2003/04 season, The Shire amassed just eight points from a possible 108, leaving the club 17 points adrift at the foot of the table. The defence conceded an average 3.2 goals per game – more than three times the number scored – while the die-hard fan base dwindled to an average 200 per game. 'Things are not bad, they're beyond belief,' said Ian Ramsay, chairman of the supporters' club. 'I wouldn't wish this on anybody.'

Matters were not helped by the board's decision two years ago to reduce players' wages from £30 to £10 per week. All the senior pros walked out leaving the Under 18s with the thankless task of holding – or more accurately surrendering – the fort. In the process the club has become the laughing stock of Scottish football, with pools punters forever marking them down to lose.

'East Stirlingshire are a tiny club but have already cost us millions this year,' said a spokesman for betting chain Ladbrokes. 'They are a banker on the coupon every week and more people back them to lose than Celtic [Scottish champions] to win. People from the UK and the world are backing whoever plays against them.'

Although there's no prospect of an end to the misery – you can't be relegated from the third division – Ian Ramsay is looking on the bright side. 'Other fans make fun of our players, but not of us,' he said. 'They think we must be amazing fans for staying loyal to such an appalling team.'

Scottish football authorities should consider enforcing measures similar to those in the Sheffield and District Junior League, where newspaper match reports are banned if one side scores more than 14. According to the *Derbyshire Times*, which described one 29–0 win as a 'comprehensive trouncing', the rule is to stop losers feeling humiliated. Sounds just the ticket for The Shire.

– CHATROOM CHARLIES –

Seven out of every ten Internet users under the age of 24 log in to chatrooms.

The aim of being linked up to an Internet chatroom is to converse and, let's be honest, flirt with other users while being in a place of safety. However, that doesn't stop women feeling vulnerable even when they are sitting in their living rooms. A survey in 16 countries, compiled by market researchers Ipsos-Reid in 2001, revealed that up to one-quarter of young women felt threatened or upset after chatroom encounters. Girls are twice as likely as boys to have uninvited comments of a sexual nature fired off at them and to be plagued with requests to meet.

But statistics are sometimes misleading, as 28-year-old Yorkshireman Trevor Tasker will vouch. He is male and over the age of 24, but that didn't stop an Internet nightmare of epic proportions unfolding. When he began an Internet chatroom relationship with a woman from South Carolina in the USA he believed he had found love at last with a woman in a million. His ardour was heightened when he received a saucy picture of Wynema Faye Shumate.

But when he got off the plane in Charleston hoping to meet the woman of his dreams, he found her some 30 years older than he had expected. Aged 65, Shumate had chosen to dispatch a photo of herself as a young woman.

Things got even worse for Tasker when he politely accepted an invitation to her house. There he eventually looked in the freezer and discovered the body of Shumate's former housemate Jim O'Neil. Although Jim's death a year previously had been from natural causes, Shumate had tried to sever his leg with an axe in order to fit his body into the freezer.

Shumate was jailed for fraud and for unlawful removal of a dead body. Tasker flew home to his mother saying: 'When I saw her picture I thought "wow". But when she met me at the airport I almost had a heart attack. I'll never log on again, looking for a dream lover.'

– CANNY PUNT –

Talking of tickets and Scottish football, don't make the mistake one pools punter made in 1992 when he altered his coupon in an attempt to convince Ladbrokes he'd correctly predicted all 61 results in the Boxing Day English and Scottish league programme. His stake was 50p, and Ladbrokes calculated that, if he was right, he'd won £3,826 billion: ten times Britain's gross national product and 65 times the nation's annual tax revenue. The punter later pleaded guilty to forgery.

– WHINING AND DINING –

British government ministers spend £31,000 a day on entertaining.

Britain's Labour government, led by Tony Blair, has been known to take the biscuit...but crumbs, its hospitality bill has now assumed banquet proportions. In the year ending April 2004, the cost of government ministers wining and dining with counterparts or contacts came to £11,446,103 – a mighty 59 per cent greater than the equivalent when Labour came to power in 1997. Worst offender was the Ministry of Defence, alone responsible for £7.9 million of the final tally. This was, apparently, the price of diplomacy in the wake of the Iraq situation. Liberal Democrat Treasury spokesman David Laws was given the figures during Parliamentary questions. He said: 'At a time when [Chancellor] Gordon Brown is looking for savings to fund his spending round, this is an obvious area where he should be wielding the axe.'

– SHOW ME THE MONEY –

The average salary in the UK is £24,440.

The expansion of the European Union in 2004 caused a huge hoo-hah in sections of the British press. Perceived wisdom suggested that 72 million new EU citizens – all from the poorer states of Eastern Europe – would soon be flooding into the UK to milk an economy where the average annual wage is £24,440 and unemployment just 4.8 per cent.

On the face of it, the doom-mongers had a point. The table at right shows the population, average wage and unemployment rate of the ten new nations as of May 2004. (Unemployment statistics for Cyprus and Malta vary by the season.)

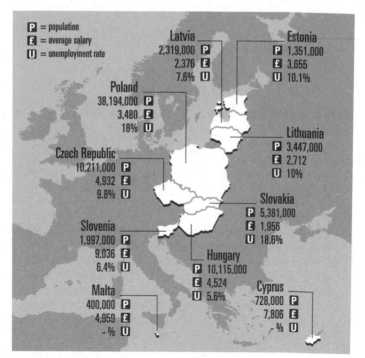

P = population
£ = average salary
U = unemployment rate

Latvia
P 2,319,000
£ 2,376
U 7.6%

Estonia
P 1,351,000
£ 3,655
U 10.1%

Poland
P 38,194,000
£ 3,480
U 18%

Lithuania
P 3,447,000
£ 2,712
U 10%

Czech Republic
P 10,211,000
£ 4,932
U 9.8%

Slovakia
P 5,381,000
£ 1,956
U 18.6%

Slovenia
P 1,997,000
£ 9,036
U 6.4%

Hungary
P 10,115,000
£ 4,524
U 5.6%

Malta
P 400,000
£ 4,959
U – %

Cyprus
P 728,000
£ 7,806
U – %

Country	Pop. (millions)	Average Salary (£s)	Unemployment Rate
Poland	38.60	3,480	18.0
Czech Republic	10.20	4,932	9.8
Hungary	10.00	4,524	5.6
Slovakia	5.43	1,956	18.6
Lithuania	3.60	2,712	10.0
Latvia	2.30	2,376	7.6
Slovenia	1.90	9,036	6.4
Estonia	1.35	3,655	10.1
Cyprus	0.76	7,806	-
Malta	0.40	4,959	-

Political hubris means that statistics on Europe-wide migration rates must be handled like glowing coals. The British government predicts on average 13,000 workers per year will move from the new states to the UK. The EU puts the figure at 17,226, while the UK group Migrantwatch, which wants immigration limited, reckons on 40,000. Take your pick.

The hard facts are that 89,000 EU migrants moved to Britain in 2002, with 125,000 Britons going the other way. There are around half a million unfilled job vacancies in the UK at any one time.

– HOURGLASS GIRLS –

Women with large breasts and narrow waists may find it easier to fall pregnant, according to researchers at Harvard University. Writing in the Royal Society journal *Proceedings B* (and doesn't that title just blow you away), they found that women with the classic hourglass look had on average 26 per cent higher levels of the hormone E2, along with enhanced levels of progesterone – both linked to fertility.

– TRIES HARD, COULD DO BETTER –

Twenty-eight per cent of a football goal's area is considered 'unsaveable'.

According to experts at England's Bath University, football players can improve their chances of scoring after being awarded a penalty with a bit of practice and placement. The most likely place to score with a penalty is a narrow band on each side of the goal at the bottom, gradually extending to wider areas at the top. Imagine a semi-circle superimposed centrally in the rectangular goal and visualise the areas outside the half moon but inside the posts. Then you'll have some idea of the shape we are talking about. It took five years for the 'unstoppable penalties' study to be concluded. Another key result from it was that more than 85 per cent of penalties are placed in the same direction as the kicker's non-kicking foot.

Professors also came up with sound advice for those teams destined for penalty shoot-outs, the lottery that decides the outcome of crunch matches in major tournaments. Teams are advised to start with their weakest players and build up to the strongest, while managers are told to rehearse penalty shoot-outs at the end of training sessions so players' legs are as tired as they would be following a match and extra time.

For the record, in the penalty shoot-out that followed the England–Portugal match in Euro 2004, when David Beckham and Rui Costa missed scoring opportunities, four of the six penalties struck by Portuguese players went into the unstoppable zone, compared with just one out of five from England.

Brazilian soccer star Ronaldinho might do well to cast his eye over the research, too. He is remembered with some bile among English football fans after his lobbed shot floated past goalie David Seaman and put England out of the 2002 World Cup. There was smug satisfaction in the English camp then when it was reported that he messed up an overhead scissor kick during the filming of an advertisement and sent a ball crashing through the window of a 12th-century cathedral. A nasty moment – even if the glass was a modern addition to the shrine of Santiago de Compostela in Spain. Director Emil Samper did the noble thing when he told a local newspaper: 'It was my fault. I asked Ronaldinho to hit the ball as hard as he could and he had the bad luck to hit the window.'

– TOO MUCH TIME –

According to market research carried out by a British insurance company, one in five pensioners returns to work following their retirement to alleviate boredom.

– TERRIBLE TAN –

Fewer than six out of ten British women use protective suncreams.

Sun-worshippers in Britain are turning their backs on products that could literally save their skins. A survey in 2004 discovered that just 59 per cent of women used oils and creams to shield the sun's harmful rays, against 70 per cent in a survey taken three years earlier. The Mintel report discovered the statistics were worse among men, as only 45 per cent now slapped on sun lotion, compared with 57 per cent in 2001.

In response, Cancer Research UK revealed the number of malignant melanoma cases – skin cancer to you and me –

reported between 1995 and 2000 rose by almost a quarter to nearly 7,000. The present death rate is running at about 2,000 a year – twice that of Australia where a sun-awareness campaign has been in full swing for 20 years.

The British reluctance to use the various lotions and potions out there may be due to a loss of faith in suncreams, with recent reports claiming a large proportion did not do exactly what they said on the bottle. A survey by the Trading Standards Institute, complete with tests carried out at independent laboratories, showed that three out of eight creams failed to protect against UVA rays that cause long-term skin damage, while four out of eight did not offer protection against cancer-causing UVB rays. Institute chief executive Ron Gainsford said: 'It seems crazy that in the UK and Europe suncreams are afforded the same regulatory status as lipsticks. In the US and Australia the industry is much more strictly controlled.'

This is bad enough, but doctors have now identified a new condition which they've nicknamed 'tanorexia', a play on the compulsive slimming disease 'anorexia'. Tanorexia is a psychological need to keep topping up your tan on sunbeds. One apparent sufferer, 13-year-old Hayley Barlow of Liverpool, explained why she secretly attends tanning parlours up to five times per week: 'When I came back from holiday with a tan everyone said I looked good,' she told the *Mail On Sunday* in May 2004. 'So last year I started using a lot of fake tan, but that made me look very orange. Then I discovered sunbeds. Now I like them so much that if I haven't gone on one for a day or so I feel white.'

It all indicates a rise in the number of red necks in the world. The phrase is generally applied to an angry young man from the American South. In fact it originated with those who worked outdoors in the sunshine who might have been protected by a hat or cap but left their neck exposed until it became dark red and positively crusty.

– IT'S A SMALL, SMALL WORLD –

More than one in ten Britons who went overseas in 2001 went to France.

The French have got a reputation for being, shall we say, curmudgeonly. They eat the limbs of cute amphibians, they are unfaithful husbands and they value obstinacy alongside those virtues of liberty and equality.

But notwithstanding all of the above, France remains the world's most popular tourist destination. In 2001, 76.5 million visitors went there, according to the World Tourism Organisation. That's 11 per cent of travellers that year.

Ranked second in the most popular international destinations is neighbouring Spain, which grabbed more than 7 per cent of globetrotters during 2001.

– JUST SAY NO? –

Nearly nine out of every ten teenagers who pledge to stay a virgin until they marry have sex within 18 months.

The alarmingly high rate of teenage pregnancies in the USA and Britain, coupled with an epidemic in sexually transmitted diseases, has brought about an evangelical response for concerned adults.

The much-publicised 'silver ring thing' centred on a public declaration by young people that they would abstain from sex before marriage. Some 2.5 million Americans took the pledge before the 'silver ring thing' roadshow came to Britain in 2004. Founder Denny Pattyn explained: 'Abstinence is the only way truly to protect yourself against getting a sexually transmitted disease, especially as a teenager.' He believes that encouraging young people to say no to sex is preferable and more effective than a sex education programme. If only it were that simple.

A study by Columbia University that investigated sexual behaviour among the young is now casting doubt on the wisdom of his words. A group of 12,000 teens and tweens were quizzed about their sexual ambitions and then re-interviewed six years later. Almost all of those who had not taken the pledge had experienced sex before marriage. The figure was slightly lower among those who had promised abstinence, at 88 per cent. More worrying, though, was the fact that those who had once adhered to the 'silver ring thing' principles, but changed tack within a few years, were less likely to use contraception.

The grown-ups have been left scratching their heads in the UK, too, as they ponder what to do about sexual precociousness. The government began an initiative optimistically called the Teenage Pregnancy Strategy in 1999 to cut the number of gymslip mums, which included dishing out free morning-after pills in some areas.

Now research by Nottingham University Business School reveals that the free pills have had no impact on teenage pregnancy rates – but appear to have made a massive contribution to the numbers suffering from sexually transmitted diseases.

Professor David Paton explained: 'There has been no drop in the rate of pregnancies. But it seems young people who know they can get the morning-after pill from school are prepared to take more risks when having sex, exposing themselves to sexual disease.'

'What's to be done?' was a question parents and professionals were left asking shortly after it was revealed that the spread of sexually transmitted diseases had risen by almost a quarter in five years in the UK. Answers on a postcard please.

– MOOSE ON THE LOOSE –

In Sweden an average of ten car crashes a day are caused by moose.

The Swedish moose (which lovers of sophistry will tell you is actually the European elk) has a tough old life considering it is free to roam a vast, sparsely-populated country which is closed most of the year. Government figures show that up to a third of Sweden's 250,000-strong wild herd are killed during the hunting season, while an average of ten car accidents per day are directly attributed to this lovable ungulate [a hoofed mammal].

Of course, the moose aren't actually driving the cars. It is worth clarifying this point because in May 2004 the BBC News website ran a story headlined 'Swedish moose steals bicycle'. This recounted the tale of Droopy Ear, a female that regularly snacked on flowers grown by Björn and Monica Helamb in their garden at Vuoggatjalme. Apparently the Helambs got so moosed-off with this that they parked a bicycle in front of their roses as a makeshift deterrent. Undeterred, Droopy Ear tucked in as usual, making her getaway with the bike hanging around her neck. It was later found abandoned and damaged beyond repair.

But then moose have always had a reputation for being awkward customers. Back in the 18th century, Swedish cavalry officers had the bright idea of using them instead of horses to ride into battle. They discovered the moose had better stamina, could cope with rougher terrain and was equally easy to train. There was just one snag. Moose don't like guns. Result? Cavalry charges went the wrong way.

– UNDER MY THUMB –

The phrase 'rule of thumb', meaning ground rule, has been attributed with numerous roots, the most likely being that old English law permitting men to beat their wives – providing the weapon was no more substantial than the width of his thumb.

– THE DEBT TO SELF-PLEASURE –

One man in three will be diagnosed with cancer – but masturbation cuts the odds.

There's bad, good and *really* good news for all you health-conscious guys. The bad comes via a study showing major differences between the sexes in death rates caused by so-called 'shared' cancers (ie those affecting both men and women). Men have double the risk of developing nine out of the ten most common types, such as lung, kidney and stomach cancer.

Research by the Men's Health Forum published in June 2004 showed that, on average, 134,000 men in the UK are diagnosed with cancer every year, producing an annual death toll of 80,000. One man in three will get the disease and a quarter of these patients will die from it. Men from poor social backgrounds fare even worse because they're twice as likely to succumb as the well-off. This all adds up to cancer being the biggest single killer of men in Britain, overtaking even heart disease. As Peter Baker, director of the MHF, puts it: 'The statistics couldn't be clearer. Men are at far greater risk of developing and dying from cancer than women.'

Part of the problem seems to lie in a peculiarly male approach to health. The MHF says men have 'specific attitudes and behaviours' concerning smoking, alcohol, diet and health education messages and are more reluctant to seek help. Which is a delicate way of saying what everyone knows anyway: that they are wheezing, drunken, fat, macho numbskulls. Besides which, their idea of exercise is to grab a box of Kleenex, tap 'extreme porn' into Google and indulge in what Americans like to call 'spanking the monkey'.

But, what's this? Masturbation is now *officially* a great way to fight prostate cancer, which, at an average 380 cases per week, is the most common form of the disease among British men. Scientists at the Cancer Council Victoria in Melbourne, Australia, compared the masturbation habits of 1,079 prostate cancer sufferers and 1,259 healthy men. They found that men in their 20s who ejaculated more than five times a week were a third less likely to develop an aggressive form of the disease.

The findings, since confirmed by a US study of 29,000 men, contradict research showing that frequent sexual intercourse *increases* the prostate cancer risk. This is thought to be because some sexually transmitted infections trigger the disease – a risk factor eliminated in masturbation.

Scientists are recommending one 'episode' per day for maximum protection on the basis that this reduces the number of carcinogens in the prostatic fluid. 'The more you flush the ducts out the less there is to hang around and damage the cells that line them,' Graham Giles, head of the

Aussie study told *New Scientist* magazine. Anthony Smith, of the Australian Research Centre in Sex, Health and Society at La Trobe University, Melbourne, said: 'If these findings hold up then it's perfectly reasonable that men should be encouraged to masturbate.'

So that's the good news. The *really* good news is that a paper presented to the American Association for Cancer Research reports that doing housework can reduce a woman's risk of endometrial cancer by an average 30 per cent. And we're not talking a quick flick round with a duster here. No siree! The best protection was seen among women who did *four hours* of chores a day or more. So guys really are doing their womenfolk a favour when they let them do all the chores.

So, the health message for couples is clear. As far as possible, she should snap on the rubber gloves, get down on all fours and scrub the floor. He meanwhile should masturbate on the sofa at a discreet distance. And maybe crack a beer or two to relax between cancer-fighting therapy.

You can't argue with science – can you?

– SIZE DOES MATTER –

A racehorse can accelerate from 0–65 kilometres per hour (0–40 mph) in under 5 seconds. A Ferrari F50 manages it in 2.5 seconds. But they both eat dirt alongside the average race-trained greyhound, which can hit the 65 kph (40 mph) mark in an incredible 1.5 seconds. In a horse versus hound race at Kempton Park in June 2004, a seven-year-old male greyhound called Simply Fabulous beat a seven-year-old gelding, Tiny Tim, by 1.34 seconds over two furlongs (a quarter of a mile), recording a time of 23.29 seconds.

– THE REAL THING –

Men who have sex twice or more a week reduce their risk of catching a cold.

Here's another statistic with which to beat the wife. A study carried out by Queens University in Belfast followed the lives and deaths of 1,000 men over a decade. Sensationally, researchers discovered that men who reported the highest orgasm rate were dropping dead at half the rate of those who didn't. It is presumed that sex contributed to weight loss and overall fitness, burning up several hundred calories in the process and raising the pulse rate just as a spell on a treadmill might do. There's a general sense of well-being that goes with regular sex, especially prevalent in those who are doing it for health reasons. Adding some more statistics into the mix, researchers at Wilkes University in Pennsylvania believe that twice-weekly sex helps to fend off colds and flu, thanks to the increase in an antibody that benefits the immune system. More sex means greater amounts of testosterone rushing through the body, improving the condition of bones and muscle. A study published by the *British Journal of Urology International* affirms that men in their 20s can reduce their chance of prostate cancer by a third if they ejaculate more than five times in a week.

But it probably is worth saying that constant sexual activity, say, after taking some performance enhancing drug, does endanger your willy. That's because penises are under pressure during erections and no blood, therefore no oxygen, goes there. Only when it is flaccid again can the muscle tissues get access to the oxygen needed to replenish cells. Without indulging in technical terms, prolonged erections are a bad thing.

– BEAR'S BREAKFAST–

About a fifth of the brown bears living in Russia's Kamchatka region is unlawfully killed each year.

Bear hunting is big business. There's hardly an organ in the poor animal's body that doesn't have some allegedly miraculous medicinal quality in the eastern Asia quack medicines market. No surprise then that poachers – and officials – are cashing in.

Assuming the above estimate is right, the bear population – around 10,000 in 2003 – will be unsustainable within a decade. Add in the legal trophy hunters who have turned Kamchatka into the number one bear-hunting destination in Russia and it's clear that time is short.

Which perhaps explains why the death of a well-known hunter, Vladimir Mamontov, in 2004 was covered with such smug satisfaction in the world's press. Mamontov, a past winner of Russia's 'Distinguished Hunter' title, apparently owned a pet bear called Horatio that he kept chained up outside his home in Tambov, central Russia. Police said he treated it cruelly and used it to practise his stalking methods.

A week after Mamontov appeared as guest of honour at the Tambov Regional Hunting Society's 115th anniversary party, Horatio took revenge. He grabbed Mamontov during feeding time, beat him round the head, broke his arms and ate him. As a police spokesman put it: 'This was some kind of divine justice – he went to feed the bear and it decided he was lunch.'

– WHAT TANGLED WEBS WE WEAVE –

Once women used to spend hours on a spinning wheel, working to get threads from fleeces. To pass the time, they would tell one another stories and probably tried to outdo one another in the process. Hence the phrase 'spinning a yarn'.

– BREAKFAST DELIVERY –

On average, ten meteorites the size of a tennis ball hit the Earth's surface every week.

Meteors are usually small chunks of space rock formed when two or more asteroids (bigger space rocks) crash together. The vast majority burn up in the Earth's upper atmosphere, the result of air drag and friction, occasionally resulting in spectacular 'shooting star' displays. Most of the 500 tennis ball-sized specimens that do get through each year fall into the sea or on to remote countryside. Very rarely, they land uncomfortably close to people. Specifically, 12-month-old Luca Archer.

In June 2004 Luca's grandmother Brenda Archer was cooking at home in Auckland, New Zealand, when a huge explosion rocked the house. As the dust cleared, her husband Phil spotted a round, smooth rock under the computer table – a disturbingly *hot* rock.

'I was in the kitchen doing breakfast about 9.30am and there was this almighty explosion,' said Brenda. 'It was like a bomb had gone off. I couldn't see anything. There was just dust. Then Phil saw a stone under the computer and it was hot to touch.'

Further investigation revealed that the meteorite had crashed through the roof, living room ceiling and sofa. At the point of impact its speed would have been around 100 metres (110 yards) per second. 'I'm just glad that no one was sitting on the couch because they would have got absolutely crowned,' observed Brenda. Of Luca, who'd been playing beside the sofa seconds earlier, she said: 'He must have a guardian angel.'

Eight out of every ten meteorites which hit Earth are chrondites, mineral balls formed around 4.6 billion years ago. The 1.3 kg (2 lb 14 oz) Auckland specimen – only the ninth ever found in New Zealand – is thought to be worth several thousand pounds to collectors.

– PET HORROR –

Three out of every 100 pets in Moscow are hooked on hard drink.

What is it with Russians and pets? Animal welfare groups in Moscow reckon 3 per cent of the city's pet population is addicted to alcohol, with one 2003 study revealing that 15 dogs died after being given vodka by their owners. Local vets have responded by offering regular 'drying out' surgeries.

Naturally there *are* times when the prospect of faithful old Roverski being well and truly mullahed is attractive. This must certainly have been true for a Russian man from Chelyabinsk, near the Ural Mountains, who spent long hours teaching his Staffordshire bull terrier to be a ferocious guard dog. When the man suffered a heart attack at home the snarling hound decided to protect him from paramedics attempting to administer life-saving drugs.

'The doctors had to call the police and our officers shot the dog,' said regional police chief Andrei Rudomyotov. 'But by the time the doctors could get in the patient was dead.'

– GOT BALLS? –

Since 1947 global sales of Subbuteo table football players have averaged nine million units per year.

Owning a Subbuteo table football set has long been a rite of passage for true footy fans. What better way to idle away the hours than zipping up your anorak and pitting your Catenaccio or W M formation against your opponent's 4-4-2 or trendy midfield 'diamond'?

Scoff if you like, but in the pre-Playstation golden age of football games, an average 300,000 of the miniature plastic teams were sold every year. In fact, since Subbuteo was invented by ornithologist Peter Adolph in 1947 (he got the name Subbuteo from the Latin word for hobby hawk), more than 500 million individual figures have been produced. By the late 1980s, international tournaments had become so lucrative that 16-year-old Justin Finch of Coventry – then ranked world number five – insured his 'flicking hand' for £160,000.

Even today, Subbuteo's manufacturer Hasbro reckons to shift around 50,000 sets a year in the UK. You can buy accessories such as referees, physios, managers, chairmen, players' wives, TV cameramen, supporters, pie and programme sellers and – since 2004 – naked pitch-invaders. Both male and female streakers are produced by Tom Taylor and his wife Sue (a former English table football champion), from their shop in Knighton, mid-Wales. So far they've sold 6,000 sets, complete with chasing policemen. A special edition has the cop holding his helmet over the streaker's rude parts.

'In real life a streaker comes onto the pitch and it's of no advantage to anyone. But in Subbuteo you can bring your streaker on – it disrupts play and it can be to your advantage,' said Tom. 'They've got all the bits. To me it's not offensive, we're all like that underneath.'

Streaking at proper football matches can occasionally be more entertaining than the game – especially if one of the centre-halves is a cop. In 2004 a naked man dashed onto Altrincham's Moss Lane ground during the Unibond Cheshire Senior Cup Final between amateur sides Witton Albion and Woodley Sports. He was promptly brought down in classic style by off-duty policeman and Witton central defender Brian Pritchard. Sadly for Pritchard the ref decided this was violent conduct and sent the officer cum player for an early bath. His ten-man side went on to lose 2–1.

– DON'T FENCE ME IN –

It's tempting to believe that being 'beyond the pale' has something to do with having a deathly pallor. In fact, pale is not only a description of colour – or lack of it – but also means a pointed piece of wood used in fencing. The phrase came into being when the English were in control of Dublin, which was defined by clearly marked boundaries from the rest of Ireland. The English stayed within the pale while the rest of the country was beyond the pale: that was, outside the confines of what was then held by the occupying forces to be decent behaviour.

From a similar era comes the word 'boycott'. This comes out of the notoriety of one Captain Boycott, a landlord's agent in County Mayo, Ireland, who insisted rents were paid by tenants in full, even if they were hard-hit by famine. Anyone in arrears on his watch was evicted – and probably starved to death soon afterwards. Before long his staff refused to work for him and Boycott was boycotted.

– TOUGH QUESTIONS –

It costs an average £129,108 to privately educate a child.

With straight 'As' at A-level considered a must by pushy parents across Britain, fee-paying schools are rubbing their hands with glee. In 2003/04 the number of pupils in private education rose for the ninth successive year to a record 508,027 – 0.1 per cent more than 2002/03 – even though fees rocketed by an average 9.6 per cent, roughly three times the inflation rate.

More than 50 schools have now broken the £20,000-a-year barrier on fees, and parents pay an average £9,222 a year to give their little darlings a 'decent' education (the figure includes both day and boarding schools). This means the average cost of educating a child privately for 14 years works out at £129,108 – and that's without the uniform, sports gear and winter ski trips to the Rockies.

Research published in 2004 by the Higher Education Careers Services Unit shows that male graduates in their late 30s earn an average of £18 per hour, £4 more than employees with mere A-levels, while for women the figure is £14, again £4 up on the A-level rate. The ultimate goal for upwardly-mobile school leavers is, naturally, a place at the elite red brick universities of Oxford and Cambridge. Yet Oxbridge is so overwhelmed with candidates waving A-grade certificates that more than 10,000 of them were rejected in 2003.

Interviewing professors have taken to asking wacky questions to sort creative free-thinkers from workaholic parent-pleasers. Examples include: 'Name Santa's reindeers?' asked of a would-be medical student; 'What's the point of me teaching you?' put to an English applicant; and 'Why do people want economic growth if money doesn't make them happy?' pondered by a prospective economics student.

While these tactics say something about Oxbridge's mentally semi-detached academics (when did you last hear drinkers in your local arguing for more economic growth), it's certainly enough to panic ambitious parents. After all, when you've spent 130k getting Rupert his interview at King's, the last thing you need is some pipe-puffing tweedy type to scupper his chances with a killer question on the Seven Dwarfs.

As a result, a new form of private tuition has emerged aimed specifically at preparing Oxbridge candidates to 'think outside the box' during their interview. One London-based company, Oxbridge Applications (which revealed the questions above), claims an average 48 per cent success rate among its candidates.

Meanwhile true free-thinkers will take heart from the urban myths growing around the Oxbridge admissions system. The best known concerns the candidate who, when asked to 'surprise' his interviewer, leant forward, flicked a lighter and set fire to the man's newspaper. Another applicant, asked to describe bravery, replied simply: 'This', and walked out.

– ATOLL ORDER –

Where did the bikini get its name? In 1946 the USA began to test atom and hydrogen bombs in the Marshall Islands, where one of the islets is called Bikini Atoll. The following year skimpy two-piece costumes were created. The public response to both events was a jaw-dropping 'wow', thus the costume was named for the benighted Central Pacific island.

– SKODA STYLE –

For decades the Czech-based car manufacturer Skoda has suffered the same old jerry-built jokes. Not any more. In 2004 Europe's most extensive consumer survey, carried out by *What Car?* magazine and the JD Power research group, revealed that Skoda came second out of 33 marques on quality, reliability, attractiveness and economy.

Skoda scored 85.2 per cent on the satisfaction scale, compared with an industry average of 79.7 per cent. That puts it ahead of Toyota (4th), BMW (6th), Volvo (8th), Jaguar (13th), Mercedes (21st) and Alfa Romeo (33rd). It's good news for the company's bosses who have never much bothered with the meaningless PR-speak that infests car marketing. Brand director Chris Craft has even compared Skodas to Marmite. 'You either love us or hate us,' he once said. 'We are not just out there existing. That would be boring.'

– GAMES TEACHERS PLAY –

Bad behaviour by students sitting exams has risen by 60 per cent.

Teachers hate exams as much as the kids. This isn't just because some pupils cheat, swear and fool around (although the Oxford, Cambridge and RSA Examinations board reported that 'malpractice' incidents rose by 60 per cent from 648 to 1,041 in 2003), but because being an invigilator is so darned boring.

Perhaps this is why teachers pass the time with juvenile practices of their own. According to a chatroom operated by the *Times Educational Supplement,* games played by invigilators include the following:

Ugly: The invigilator stands next to the ugliest pupil in the room until he or she makes eye contact.

Good Kid, Bad Kid: A teacher highlights a pupil from his or her class on the exam attendance grid. The other invigilator has to guess which category of kid.

On Your Marks: Teachers walk quickly (but quietly) around the exam hall and record their personal-best times.

Paper Chase: Won by the invigilator who hands out most sheets of spare paper. 'You start having veritable sprints between you to get to bewildered kids, or cleverly handing out reams of paper to a kid who only wanted advice,' one chatroom contributor wrote.

Chicken: Only for the stout-hearted. Teachers deliberately walk between desks towards an advancing colleague. The loser is the first to dodge out of the way.

– ANATOMY OF A SNACK –

The notion of a 'sandwich' was created by John Montagu, the fourth Earl of Sandwich, who urged his servants to provide a swift, tasty snack – in an era when eating was a far more formal and time-consuming affair – in order that he could remain at the gaming tables for longer. The result was sliced beef between two pieces of bread, and Montagu was seen so often with one in his hand that the culinary creation took his name.

– UNREAL HISTORY –

One in ten people believe Hitler never existed.

For a nation with such a long and proud history, the Brits are real numbskulls when it comes to possessing historical knowledge. A survey of 2,000 visitors to Blenheim Palace showed that half believed Nelson commanded British troops at Waterloo, half thought King Arthur existed, one in seven reckoned the Battle of Hastings was fictitious and one in five had Harold Wilson, not Churchill, down as Britain's wartime prime minister.

It gets worse. One in 20 thought Conan the Barbarian, a role played by Arnold Schwarzenegger, was a real person, while some wrote that both Lord Edmund Blackadder and Xena, Warrior Princess (both characters from TV) were real historical figures. And then, perhaps most bizarre of all, there are the views on Adolf Hitler...

The mention of Adolf brings to mind one of the world's most unusual sporting trophies – the Hitler Cup – an amber-encrusted brass salver commissioned by the Führer as top prize for an amateur international golf foursomes competition staged in Baden-Baden immediately after the 1936 Berlin Olympic Games.

Hitler, you'll recall, had been mightily cheesed off to watch American Jesse Owens humble the cream of Aryan athletes. He was counting on better things at Baden-Baden and was delighted to learn that the German pairing of Leonard von Beckerath and CA Helmers were top of the leaderboard after two rounds. Hitler headed south to present his trophy personally.

But golf's a funny old game and England's Tommy Thirsk and Arnold Bentley carded 65s in two sensational final rounds. Hitler got the hump, refused to present the trophy and drove straight back to Berlin. The cup eventually ended up in London's Golfers' Club and is now owned by a property company. Tommy Thirsk went on to captain England 30 times and notched 13 holes-in-one during his career.

– O BROTHER, HOW MUCH ART THOU? –

The average price of the top ten most expensive artworks is $65.92 million.

What's the best investment ever? A leading contender has to be *Garçon à la Pipe* painted by Pablo Picasso in 1905. The picture was bought by former US ambassador to Britain, John Whitney, in 1950 for $30,000 dollars. It was sold at Sotheby's, New York, for $104 million in May 2004. Leaving aside inflation, this means the painting has increased in value by an average $5,322 per day.

In the all-time most expensive paintings chart, Pablo has not only gone-in-with-a-bullet at number one, he also has three other works in the top ten. Since you ask, here's the list in question:

1 *Garçon à la Pipe*, Picasso	$104m (2004)
2 *Portrait of Dr Gachet*, Van Gogh	$82.5m (1990)
3 *Bal du Moulin de la Galette*, Renoir	$78m (1990)
4 *Massacre of the Innocents*, Rubens	$76.7m (2002)
5 *Portrait de l'artiste sans barbe*, Van Gogh	$65m (1998)
6 *Rideau, Cruchon et Compotier*, Cezanne	$55m (1999)
7 *Les Noces de Pierrette*, Picasso	$51m (1989)
8 *Femme aux Bras Croisés*, Picasso	$50m (2000)
9 *Irises*, Van Gogh	$49m (1989)
10 *La Rêve*, Picasso	$48m (1997)

Meanwhile, modern art has created a few headlines of its own. Chilean-born artist Marco Evaristti is one of modern art's extremists. He created a stir with his Millennium exhibition at the Trapholt Art Museum in Kolding, Denmark, that comprised ten working blenders filled with water, each containing a goldfish.

The 'pièce de résistance' was an invitation proffered to art museum visitors to press the 'on' button and so create fish soup. It's believed that at least seven fish died in the blender blades before police intervened. Museum director Peter Meyer was later acquitted on animal cruelty charges.

The Top Ten Most Expensive Paintings

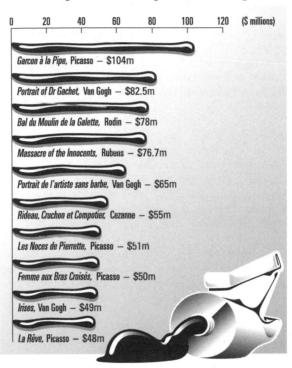

0   20   40   60   80   100   120   ($ millions)

Garcon à la Pipe, Picasso — $104m

Portrait of Dr Gachet, Van Gogh — $82.5m

Bal du Moulin de la Galette, Rodin — $78m

Massacre of the Innocents, Rubens — $76.7m

Portrait de l'artiste sans barbe, Van Gogh — $65m

Rideau, Cruchon et Compotier, Cezanne — $55m

Les Noces de Pierrette, Picasso — $51m

Femme aux Bras Croisés, Picasso — $50m

Irises, Van Gogh — $49m

La Rêve, Picasso — $48m

In 2004 Evaristti was wowing the public again, this time by painting the tip of a Greenland iceberg red. To do so he employed the services of two icebreakers, their 20-man crews, three fire hoses and 3,000 litres (660 US gallons) of paint. Perhaps it wasn't the word 'wow' forming on the lips of art lovers everywhere, but the word 'why'.

He explained: 'We all have a need to decorate Mother Nature because it belongs to us all.' Naturally.

– TAKE YOUR PICKLE –

An average German eats 1.8 kg (4 lb) of sauerkraut per year.

Sauerkraut has traditionally been of use only for German-baiting exercises by stand-up comics and tabloid sub-editors. Now there's a real danger that the British will start eating the stuff. The Association of European Sauerkraut Producers wants to educate all European palates to the delights of their traditional pickled cabbage dish.

During the First World War, phenomenal sauerkraut consumption earned Germans the nickname 'krauts' among American troops. Even today they eat an average 1.8 kg (4 lb) per head of the country's total 105,000-tonne annual output. However sales have steadily slipped and the AESP is trying to shore things up with a recipe guide showing the versatility of the hallowed veg. It can apparently be served in pizzas, cakes and even sorbet.

'There are some parts of Europe that are simply underdeveloped and urgently need sauerkraut development aid,' said Association chairman Eckart Hengstenberg. 'Our aim is to move sauerkraut away from its antiquated image and give it a new, progressive and modern image.'

– CALIFORNIA BREATHIN' –

Of the 32 million passenger cars sold in America every year, around one in eight are bought in California.

That means 4 million new cars a year for the Golden State. Because of the effect exhaust fumes have on air quality, California is the only state allowed to set its own vehicle pollution limits, although to date these have tended to follow federal law.

However, Californian legislators are fast losing patience with Washington and want car manufacturers to slash carbon dioxide emissions by a third inside 11 years. No country – never mind state – has ever taken on the powerful automotive industry over greenhouse gases, and politicians from all sides are watching closely. The car industry says California's plans would add £600 ($1,100) to the cost of an average car and warns of litigation. The state's reaction? Bring it on.

– SICKIE BUSINESS –

UK workers take an average of 7.2 sick days per year.

In the '70s, right-wing politicians and business leaders liked to condemn strike action as the 'British Disease'. Now it seems sickies – days off for no good reason – are the demon of the workplace.

According to a 2004 survey of 500 top companies by the Confederation of British Industry, UK businesses were hit for £11.6 billion in 2003 – the bill for 176 million working days lost to staff absences. This is a 6 per cent increase on the previous year and means that every worker takes, on average, 7.2 days a year off ill.

The average is higher in the public sector (8.9 days) than in private companies (6.9). It is also worse among businesses with a 5,000-plus workforce (10.2 days) than for smaller ones of 50 or fewer (4.2 days). This huge difference is attributed to the closer contact between managers and employees in small companies.

Many of the absences are genuine, although three-quarters of companies say staff do feign sickness, particularly on Mondays and Fridays (to allow a long weekend). If their suspicions are correct the CBI believes sickies account for 25 million lost days a year at a cost to employers of £1.75 billion.

– GOLF'S GLITTERING PRIZE –

Since 1980, the number of holes-in-one achieved at the US Open has risen to an average of one a year.

The prospect of hitting a hole-in-one on the golf course still seems a Utopian dream to most golfers whose games are characterised by sand-swiping, pond-plumbing and ditch-reaching drives. One insurance company puts a high-ranking professional player's chances at one in 3,756. For an amateur the figure is a bit more daunting, at one in 12,750. In fact, holes-in-one – a feature of the game since 1868, when the first ever was achieved in Scotland by one Tom Morris at the Open in Prestwick, Scotland – are not so tricky if you focus on all the anecdotal evidence.

Take the one-armed man who has netted not one but two holes-in-one. Art Baird took up golf 14 years after losing his arm in an industrial accident, primarily to strengthen his wrist. His first ace came in 1991 at Apache Junction, Arizona, and he matched it at Clovis, New Mexico, 11 years later, aged 74. 'I never played [golf] with two arms and I've never used my prosthesis when I play golf. I've had to make compensations because of the one arm but there are so few things I can't do, I can't even think of anything.'

A 101-year-old man became a record breaker in May 2001 in Florida, when he used a four iron to make a 99-metre (108-yard) par three hole in a single shot. It was nothing special to Harold Stilson, who had already achieved the feat five times before. He stole the record for the oldest golfer to do so from 99-year-old Otto Bucher, who achieved a hole in a single shot in La Manga, Spain, in 1985. The oldest woman to make a hole-in-one appears in the records as Rose Montgomery, a sprightly 96-year-old, who did so in 1992.

The statistics for the youngest to achieve the accolade are perhaps even more amazing. Five-year-old Keith Long connected cleanly with his golf club and potted a 127-metre (140-yard) hole at Jackson, Michigan, in October 1998, from the tee. Brittney Andreas was just six when she completed the 91-metre (100-yard) second hole in a single shot in Austin, Texas, in 1991. The award for the longest goes to Robert Mitera, who completed a 408-metre (446-yard) hole at the Miracle Hills Golf Club in Nebraska, USA, in one shot on 7 October 1965.

To further defy the odds, father and son golfers Peter and Christopher Haws both made a hole-in-one on the same green at Girton in Cambridgeshire in 1992. (For proper golfers everywhere, Peter was using a seven iron while Chris preferred the eight iron.)

In a similar vein, Graham King notched up a hole-in-one at a course in Wild Turkey, New York, just three days after his father John celebrated scoring his first ever hole-in-one at a course in Grimsby, England.

Clifford and Gwen Briggs both found glory at the 16th at a course in Parkstone, near Poole in Dorset, in 2000, although their triumphs occurred several hours apart. And Steve Fear became one of an elite few to score two holes-in-one during the same round in a competition at Dunstanburgh Castle Golf Club in Northumberland, England, in the summer of 2000.

On a final note, the odds of hitting a hole-in-one were stacked against Geoff Langlois in 1999 when he took to the L'Ancresse golf course in Guernsey. A man with the same name had already achieved the feat that day at the St Pierre Park golf course just 5 km (3 miles) away. But guess what? He did.

– THE GREAT HOLE-IN-ONE CAPER –

*The odds of a hole-in-one at any professional golf competition
have shrunk from the accepted norm of 6–4 or evens.*

In 1987 two former betting office managers, John Carter and Paul
Simmons from Essex, decided to try their luck as full-time
gamblers. Their research suggested big money could be made from
golf by betting that any one player would card a hole-in-one
during professional tournaments.

Big name bookies such as Corals, Ladbrokes and William Hill
knew the true odds of this feat stood at even money or 6-4. But in
the '80s golf was a fledgling gambling market. Thousands of
small-town bookies hadn't done the maths. Besides, golfers had
rapidly got an awful lot better!

Hole-in-one statistics for the US Open illustrate the point,
although the records are incomplete. In the 72 years between
1907 and 1979, just 13 HIOs were carded – one every five-and-a-
half years. Yet in the 22 years spanning 1980 and 2002 this
average was cut to one *per year*. You don't need to be a gambling
genius to see the odds shortening.

Yet, incredibly, Carter and Simmons were laid anything up to 50-
1 when they road-tested their theory. Convinced the bookies were
there for the taking, they mounted a 'deluxe' coup against some
4,000 independent betting shops in England and South Wales
early in 1991. This was run like a military exercise, requiring
hundreds of photocopied phone listings, and the purchase of
street maps, to speed things up.

All told, the partners drove 50,000 miles, varying stakes to avoid
suspicion on the bookmakers' grapevine. Carter adopted the
character of a quiet office worker living out his lifelong dream to
visit major tournaments. He would start with small bets and build
up to doubles and trebles worth more than £10,000 in potential
winnings. Simmons meanwhile was the high-rolling punter who

openly flashed his cash, throwing in 'mixer' or 'sweetener' bets on football and cricket, before casually enquiring about the golf odds. By the time the tournament season was under way they had together staked £30,000.

Almost immediately the winnings rolled in. But the *big* return rested on five 'banker' tournaments linked to multiple bets. The last of these – the European Open at Walton Heath – saw Miguel Jimenez take a single shot at the 142-metre (155-yard) 17th. It was worth £3,255 a yard to Carter and Simmons and guaranteed a total payout of £500,000.

To their credit, most bookmakers honoured the bets. Disgracefully 11 didn't, presumably relying on the argument that it's fine if bookies know the true odds – but not punters.

– DUNGEON MASTERS –

The cult game Dungeons and Dragons, which purists play using only dice, paper, pens and a vivid imagination, celebrated its 30th anniversary in 2004. Around 20 million people have tried D&D in that time, adopting fantasy character roles such as fighters, magic users, bards, druids and clerics. Mind you, the cash they've spent is real enough. It works out at $100 per head on game equipment, accessories and strategy books.

The game's inventors, Gary Gygax and Dave Arneson, originally reckoned on selling 50,000 copies. They fell out in the 1980s and sued each other over development plans. In the 1990s both sold their royalty rights to the current owner, Wizards of the Coast, which estimates that three million Americans still play the game every month.

– STICKY FINGERS –

An average of £1.2 billion worth of office property is stolen every year in the UK.

Let's face it: who hasn't occasionally 'borrowed' an envelope or a few paper clips from the boss's stationary cupboard. Obviously, it doesn't happen in the *Lore of Averages* office, but thousands of you readers *are* by your own admission sticky-fingered, cheating, rotten pilferers. A 2004 survey shows that two-thirds of British workers believe it's acceptable to steal from the office, compared with an average 49 per cent across Europe. And that runs up a bill of £1.2 billion for UK companies annually.

Mind, there's thieving and then there's fill-yer-boots-and-whoop-de-do thieving. Joyti De-Laurey falls into the latter category: an employee who has single-handedly redefined the meaning of workplace fraud on account of the £4.3 million or so she filched from her bosses at investment bankers Goldman Sachs.

Southwark Crown Court, London, heard how she was employed by the bank after her attempt to run a sandwich bar turned sour. As PA to a senior manager she was soon forging cheques and other documents to steal money from private accounts. This serviced a hugely extravagant lifestyle in which De-Laurey spent £400,000 on Cartier jewellery, £175,000 on an Aston Martin car, £150,000 on a speedboat and £750,000 on a seafront villa in Cyprus. She got seven years.

– DESERT SEX –

Around seven British soldiers per month fell pregnant while serving in Iraq during 2003. The figure is said to have raised eyebrows at the Ministry of Defence, although a spokesman said it included 'women who only discovered they were pregnant once they arrived in Iraq'.

– ROOM SELF-SERVICE –

Two-thirds of female and half of male hotel guests steal items from the room.

How can you be certain of getting great value from your weekend break? Simple. You steal shampoo, towels, ashtrays and batteries – or indeed anything that isn't nailed down among the room contents. According to the American Hotel and Lodging Association, an average $1.07 million worth of items per week 'disappear' from US hotels. The Holiday Inn chain alone reckons to lose more than 1,500 towels per day and a survey by British insurers Hill House Hammond revealed that two out of three women, and half the men, had stolen something from a hotel room.

Let's be clear: we're not talking here about a few plastic shower gel bottles and a dressing gown. Some managers tell of guests arriving with a set of screwdrivers to remove everything from the refrigerator to the toilet seat. Colin Bennett, general manager at the Sheraton Park Tower in London's Mayfair, remembers working at one hotel where bedroom artwork and electrical goods were constantly being helped from the premises.

'Looking back over the CCTV footage we would see a guest walk through a busy reception struggling under the weight of a television set, yet no one would bat an eyelid,' he said. 'As soon as I walked into the lobby of one hotel I immediately realised something was missing, but I couldn't put my finger on it. It transpired that three people had strolled into reception dressed in overalls and wheeled the grand piano out of the hotel and down the street, never to be seen again.'

– EYE FULL –

The London Eye averages 75,000 visitors per week.

London's traditional tourist hotspots have undoubtedly suffered through the threat of international terrorism and a weak global economy, with 13 per cent fewer overseas visitors. As if that wasn't bad enough, the likes of the National Gallery (average 95,000 visitors per week), the British Museum (92,000) and the Tower of London (38,500) are getting competition from two new kids on the block – the Tate Modern art gallery (67,000) and the British Airways London Eye (75,000).

For the uninitiated, by the way, the Tate Modern is an imposing landmark packed with hot and sweaty customers observing weird and wonderful sexual imagery. The London Eye is pretty much the same except the sex is for real. Honestly. So, dusty old Egyptian mummy at the British Museum? Or live sex show at 450 feet? Where would you rather go for the day?

According to the British tabloids – who have, naturally, re-christened the giant wheel the 'Mile Eye Club' – BA managers are deeply concerned about the antics of couples in the £285-a-spin 'Cupid's Capsule' (essentially your own private pod). It seems exhibitionists delight in having transparent sex high above the Thames and reckon the 20-minute trip is perfect for a quickie. So-called 'sex guards' have now been drafted onto the payroll to stop any hanky panky.

An Eye 'insider' said: 'There's a terrific thrill in having sex in a public place. But you can easily see into the pod next door as the ride goes round, and this kind of rude activity could ruin a family day out. British Airways have no option but to employ stewards to keep watch.'

– FAITH IN BART –

Times are hard for the Anglican Church, which saw the average number of UK churchgoers dip from 1,274,000 per week in 2000 to 1,166,000 in 2002. God works in strange ways though. After the Archbishop of Canterbury, Rowan Williams, praised *The Simpsons* as 'a family with remarkable strength and remarkable mutual commitment', the show's producers want to use him for a cameo role. Apparently the ultra-cynical character Comic Book Guy will call Rowan 'the worst archbishop ever'. Slated on *The Simpsons*? Now that should give the Church some street cred.

– CAR CRAZY –

In China, a BMW costs 25 times the average professional salary.

Its factories consume one-third of the world's coal, 30 per cent of its steel and 40 per cent of all cement. Unsurprisingly, there are big rewards for top businessmen and a booming market in luxury goods such as flash cars.

Some experts believe Chinese car sales will soon pass three million a year (overtaking Britain's 2.6 million) and top 20 million a year (more than the USA) by 2020. If car ownership ever reaches the same level as America, there will be 600 million cars on Chinese roads – more than currently exist in the entire world.

This is great news for manufacturers such as BMW, which has just opened a factory in the provincial city of Shenyang. A BMW series 7 saloon costs around 1.2 million yuan (£80,600), which works out at about 25 times the average professional's salary. However, the Chinese are demanding customers. According to one harassed dealer in Beijing: 'If something goes wrong under warranty, they're not interested in repairs. They want a new car.'

– COMMUTER CURSE –

Britain's railway passengers wasted 4,632 years during 2001 as a result of late trains.

British trains run late once every five journeys. So next time you're in pay talks with the boss, why not suggest the following: you'll arrive for work punctually four days out of five. On the fifth you'll get there when you can. In return you'll trouser a whopping 25 per cent annual bonus.

Sounds unlikely? Not if you're one of Network Rail's five executive directors. They together shared £400,000 in bonuses for 2004, even though their stewardship failed to meet the minimum rail punctuality target of 82 per cent. Over the previous year, trains ran on time for only 81 per cent of journeys, or four in every five. Network Rail did exceed two other targets – financial efficiency and asset stewardship – which must be a massive comfort to office late-comers as they dodge the boss's laser-like stares.

It's NR's responsibility to maintain track, tunnels and stations, allowing the privately-owned train operators to meet their timetables. Yet the operators are not entirely blameless. Shortly before NR's bonus-fest, homebound passengers who'd boarded at London's Waterloo station were mildly irritated when their train twice shuddered to a halt for no obvious reason. This turned to jaw-plunging incredulity when a guard's voice crackled over the tannoy to admit the crew was lost.

'Is there', he pleaded, 'a train driver on board who knows the way to Portsmouth?' Remember, an average £960,000 per week of *public* money was spent on the railways during 2003.

– DISTANCE EARNING –

In November 2002, 461,000 Britons – roughly one in every 125 – were enrolled in distance learning courses.

That figure is down from 639,000 in 1995. And no wonder, with outfits like UkeU. The bosses of this 'e-university' spent £30 million of a UK government grant aimed at encouraging students to study degrees online. The idea flopped when just 900 people signed up. At around £33,000 per student they could have all gone to Harvard for a year.

Despite this fiasco, lawyers advised that 31 out of UkeU's 75 employees were entitled to bonuses ranging from 10 to 50 per cent – possibly 100 per cent in some cases. When questioned on this, David Young, chairman of the Higher Education Funding Council for England, admitted that 'performance targets were rather loose'.

He told the House of Commons Select Committee: 'I am personally not very happy with what I know of the bonus scheme. But it was not something that had or required our approval.' Select committee chairman Barry Sheerman was more forthright. 'What on earth is going on when bonuses are being paid to those who have barely earned one penny piece for the company?' he said. Sounds like fertile recruiting ground for Network Rail.

– CH-CH-CHEQUE IT OUT –

The word 'exchequer' took root in the reign of King Henry I (r1100–1135), the youngest son of William the Conqueror and a canny monarch when it came to money matters. Inspired by the Middle Eastern abacus, it was a piece of chequered cloth upon which counters or cash were placed for counting by sheriffs and the like. Ultimately the chap in charge became the chancellor of the exchequer and hence the issue of money – once entirely in the hands of the king – was known as a cheque.

– THE LAST LAUGH –

The average UK burial service costs £2,048.

If you think the cost of living rises fast, try dying. A survey by the friendly society Oddfellows discovered that, between 1998 and 2000, the average price of a UK burial service rose by up to 25 per cent to £2,048. Cremation was slightly cheaper – up 12 per cent over two years to £1,215. The trend is nothing new: over the last nine years burial costs have risen by a total of 129 per cent and cremations by 67 per cent.

It really is no joke. Unless of course you're Irish, in which case death is nothing *but* a joke. Take the passing of Irish clay pigeon shooting champion Tony Mullen of Dundalk, Co. Louth, who decided his mortal remains should fly to numerous last resting places. In the final weeks of his terminal illness the 63-year-old told his family he wanted to be cremated, have his ashes ground up with bitumen and recycled as 100-mm (4-inch) diameter clay pigeons.

According to long-time friend Willie Hughes, the *craic* was to 'scatter him all over the place'. Willie added: 'When Tony knew he was ill, he brought up the idea in a jokey way among friends – he said he wanted to go out with a bang. He would talk and laugh about it and it was no problem to him.

'I told the family that I would spread Tony's ashes at every ground he had shot at in England, Ireland, Scotland and Wales. I decided to take the lead out of the cartridges and fill them with Tony's ashes so when the cartridge went off his ashes came out instead of the lead.' Willie said a more formal ceremony would be held once the recycled clays were ready so that 'each family member can get a chance to take a shot.'

Of course, not every Irishman goes to such lengths to cheer up their future mourners. The comic genius Spike Milligan, star of The Goons, had a simple seven-word Gaelic epitaph engraved on his tomb in St Thomas's churchyard, Winchelsea, East Sussex. His last laugh read: *Duirt me leat go raibh me breoite* or, in English, *I told you I was ill.*

– SHUSH, THIEVES AT WORK –

UK libraries lose an average of £150 million worth of books a year to thieves.

The quiet ones are always the worst. Studies suggest the average number of books stolen each year from UK libraries amounts to 5.3 per cent of the total stock, a loss of £150 million for taxpayers. But that's petty cash alongside the total £26 million worth of rare books snaffled by the late Frede Moeller-Kristensen, senior librarian at the Royal Danish Library.

Moeller-Kristensen and a team of four accomplices, which included his wife and son (all later jailed), stole around 3,200 literary masterpieces over three decades. They were caught after a tip-off from the London auction house Christie's, where experts had grown suspicious at the sheer number of works being offered by the family.

The final straw came when the Moeller-Kristensens sent valuers an original 1517 work by the Spanish poet Bartholome de Torres Naharro. Only two copies of the book, *Propalladia*, were known to exist and a third should comfortably have made £500,000 at auction. Trouble was, this one carried traces of an erased library stamp linking it to the RDL's royal collection.

– CHEATING GENES –

Unfaithful women are most likely to have their affairs between the ages of 31 and 40.

Around 23 per cent of women aged 18–60 admit to having an affair while in an apparently monogamous relationship, according to a study at Guy's and St Thomas' Hospital, London. However it may not be their fault. The research suggests unfaithfulness appears to be linked to an 'infidelity gene' inherited from their parents.

The researchers, led by Professor Tim Spector, compared the results of a questionnaire given to 5,000 female twins alongside those from 5,000 randomly selected women. They found that if one of a pair of twins had a tendency to sleep around, the chance that her sister would behave the same way was 55 per cent – way above the 23 per cent norm. The age at which women were most likely to stray was between 31 and 40.

It's tempting to attribute these results to the seven-year itch, the time when a relationship comes under most strain. Yet a separate study by Dr Michael Svarer at the University of Aarhus in Denmark suggests that in today's world it's more like the *two-year* itch. His analysis of 7,000 Western marriages showed the risk of a split rises rapidly in the first 18 months of wedlock, peaking after two years. After 14 years together, only one in 100 couples seek divorce.

'You go into a relationship, you gather information, and at some point you make a decision,' said Svarer. 'That point seems to be two years. If the marriage survives five years it is a good match.' The Danish research also found that couples are far more likely to experience marital problems if they don't co-habit before taking vows. One in 12 of these 'traditional' marriages fails within two years compared to one in 30 among the co-habiters.

Spector's work raises the possibility that marriage failure rates could be reduced if the gene or combination of genes responsible for unfaithfulness is isolated. Then cautious couples could simply check out each other's cheat rating before booking the lawyer for a pre-nuptial agreement, just in case.

'By studying twins we can separate nature from nurture,' Professor Spector told *The Sunday Times*. 'It does seem that there is a strong link between a woman's genetic inheritance and the chances that she will commit infidelity.' It's also possible that well over 23 per cent of women have the cheat gene. Many social scientists suspect levels of female unfaithfulness are underestimated because so many are reluctant to admit their behaviour – even anonymously.

– TV NATION –

Britons are the most watched people in the world, according to research by Professor Clive Norris, deputy director of the Centre for Criminological Research at Sheffield University. He estimates that the UK is covered by 4,285,000 closed circuit television (CCTV) cameras, an average of one for every 14 people.

Part of this strategy is supposedly to combat Britain's alcohol-fuelled yob culture, a problem not confined to the big city centres. Figures released by the Audit Commission for 2003 show that the nightclubbers of Newcastle, for instance, generate 0.8 per cent of drunken violence per 1,000 residents – just one-tenth of the figure for 'genteel' Bournemouth.

– BLEEDIN' KIDS –

Surveys show 12 children in a typical UK class of 30, and one in eight US students, are bullied.

School bullying – which for some bizarre reason is still not considered 'proper' crime – is as rampant as ever. The US National Crime Victimization Survey suggests that an average 2.7 million violent crimes take place annually either at or near schools. Half of all 6th- through 12th-grade students personally witness these and one in eight say they have been victims.

In Britain a 1999 NOP Research Group survey showed that four out of ten children suffer from bullying. Shamefully, in 22 per cent of cases when these youngsters reported their ordeal, nothing happened to the bullies. The children's charity Childline says it gets more calls about bullying than any other subject – around 60 per day.

Things are hardly much better in Japan, a country where harsh discipline and institutionalised violence has been a feature of school life for decades. Although bullying showed a 1.4 per cent decline to 30,918 cases in 2001, overall cases of school violence rose 10.4 per cent to a record 40,374.

Children's rights campaigners say the statistics are in any case unreliable. 'So-called violent kids who attack their classmates may in fact be bullying victims trying to defend themselves,' said one prominent lawyer, Sayoko Ishii. 'Many children who engage in violent activities have been subjected to physical violence by their parents or teachers.'

She's not kidding. In June 2004 the Japanese media reported the case of a 17-year-old student who was ordered to write an essay in his own blood as a punishment for falling asleep in class. His teacher gave him a boxcutter which the lad used to slice open the index finger on his left hand. He then used the wound as an inkwell.

'To ask a student to write in their own blood is something that I just can't imagine,' said Hiroaki Dan, head teacher of the school in Fukuoka, southern Japan. After delivering this damning condemnation, he allowed the maniac responsible to resume teaching. Says it all, doesn't it?

– DANK GOODNESS –

Hay fever sufferers cost Britain's National Health Service an estimated £20 million per week.

Stuffed up nose? Sneezing fits? If you're among the ten million Britons who suffer from hay fever, this next item will be a sight for sore eyes. Assuming you can read through your tears, of course.

A revolutionary new drug called R112, developed by California-based Rigel Pharmaceuticals and due to be commercially launched before 2009, is said to stop the body's immune system from producing the cocktail of chemicals responsible for hay fever symptoms. R112 does this within 15 seconds of you spraying it up your hooter. Current anti-histamine treatments manage to suppress just one of the chemicals.

UK government figures show that during the summer around 10 per cent of sufferers lose an average three hours of their working day, while one in four is forced to take time off.

– DEFINATELY RITE! –

It was the 19th-century American president Andrew Jackson who observed that 'it's a damn poor mind that can only think of one way to spell a word'. In one sense, he had a point. Ernest Hemingway was a terrible speller, offering editors delights such as 'professessional' and 'archiologist'. Virginia Woolf always used 'pannelled' for panelled and 'naiv' for naïve, while Keats bungled four times in the first ten lines of his 'Ode to Autumn'. Will Shakespeare wrote his name at least a dozen different ways, though in his day the rules of spelling hadn't been, well, spelt out.

One survey of school work highlighted by linguistics professor Vivian Cook in his book *Accomodating Brocolli in the Cemetary* shows that six out of ten British 15-year-olds can't write ten lines without at least one spelling mistake. Therefore in the spirit of educational advancement, *The Lore of Averages* has compiled a top ten handy cut-out-and-keep list of Internet howlers tested on the search engine Google. The figure shown is the approximate number of web pages found to carry the offending word.

Correct word	Spelled as...	No. of web pages with misspelling
accommodation	accomodation	3,480,000
separate	seperate	1,290,000
definitely	definately	1,230,000
receive	recieve	1,160,000
independent	independant	1,010,000
minuscule*	miniscule	231,000
ecstasy	ecstacy	209,000
liaison	liason	180,000
supersede	supercede	113,000
pronunciation	pronounciation	83,400

*Some pedants argue that miniscule is a correct variant. That would spoil our survey, so we'll gloss over it.

– HIGH GRADE COFFEE –

30 minutes of chat shows per day raises your IQ by an average of five points.

Drinking a cup of coffee and watching chat shows like *Richard And Judy* are a vital part of exam preparation, according to a survey of 200 students at Reading University. Researchers found that watching 30 minutes of TV couch banter raised IQ levels by an average of five points, while coffee added a further two. Drinking orange juice or listening to classical music produced no significant improvement, and last-minute revision actually harmed students' performance.

Professor Kevin Warwick, a cybernetics expert who led the study, said the TV and coffee routine could make the difference between passing and failing. 'We really are talking about that much effect,' he said. 'It seems that just watching a bit of television, particularly *Richard And Judy*, before you go into an exam has an amazingly positive effect on how you perform.'

Presenting his findings at a business training conference in London, Professor Warwick said caffeine was particularly useful as an antidote to 'post-lunch dips' in concentration. Its effect peaked within 30 minutes but lasted for hours. 'If you're about to make an important deal it's giving you a bit of an edge,' he said. 'What seems clear, but surprising, is that many of the so-called bad influences, such as coffee, have a positive effect on short-term performance.'

This may be unwelcome news for researchers at Brazil's State University of Campinas who have spent months screening 3,000 *Coffea arabica* trees to find some with naturally decaffeinated beans. They have isolated three from Ethiopia and are planning a breeding programme. Fears that caffeine can raise blood pressure and cause palpitations have seen decaffeinated coffee take 10 per cent of world sales, although hardened drinkers bemoan the loss of flavour.

– COUNTRY BUMPKINS –

An average 315 people per day move from British cities in search of a better life in the country, according to figures from the Countryside Agency. The influx helped push up rural wages by 4.1 per cent in 2003, compared with 2.8 per cent in the city. However the blow-ins – as friendly country folk like to call them – face an overall 9 per cent pay cut.

– FOOTY FEVER –

Illegal gambling on the Euro 2004 soccer tournament averaged £22.8 million per match in Thailand.

The Euro 2004 soccer tournament was generally bad news for Eastern Asia businesses. Gambling on European games (less likely to be rigged) is a massive industry and almost routine in countries like Cambodia, where 45 per cent of the population lives on less than $1 a day.

One Chinese survey of 3,357 people showed that a third were seeking time off work to watch Euro 2004 matches and one in five planned to buy bigger TVs. Traders on the Malaysian Stock Exchange complained that business was bleak, with bleary-eyed investors more interested in the spread-betting odds than commodity price movements.

In Thailand, where gambling is both hugely popular and illegal, the government's Soccer Gambling Suppression Centre said 37 bookies and 400 punters had been arrested in Bangkok during the first week of Euro 2004. Police estimated the illegal cash flow generated by the tournament at around $800 million, which at current exchange rates works out at £434 million or £22.8 million for each of the 19 matches.

Such is the football fanaticism in Thailand that prison officials took desperate measures to stop cons running their own underground betting rings. The most imaginative scheme was an elephants versus prisoners match at Ayuthaya Prison, north of Bangkok. This involved painting the elephants with the flags of all 16 competing European teams and the use of an over-size 9-kg (20-lb) ball. There were conflicting reports of the result, either a 5-5 draw or 7-6 to the elephants, who were ridden by their *mahouts* (handlers).

'We train the elephants every day to play soccer, kick the ball and to keep from stepping on the other people,' said Pattarapon Meepan, son of the jumbos' owner. 'They try their best.' It's not clear how many of the prisoners were stretchered off.

– BEATLING ABOUT –

During a career spanning 47 years, Sir Paul McCartney has played an annual average of nearly 65 gigs – more than one a week.

Sir Paul first took to the stage to perform as a member of The Quarry Men at Liverpool's New Clubmoor Hall on 18 October 1957. Since then he is believed to have played 2,523 times with The Beatles, 140 times with his subsequent band, Wings, and made 325 solo appearances on tour and at major events including Live Aid.

Before he began a world tour in 2004, his personal concert appearance tally stood at 2,988. So when the curtain went up on his show in St Petersburg, Russia, in June that year, he was not only celebrating his first visit to the city but also his 3,000th live appearance at the age of 62. He also holds the record for attracting the biggest ever stadium audience, at Rio de Janeiro in 1990, when 184,000 people flocked to hear him.

– HOUNDED THROUGH COURT –

Up to 100 rescued dogs a week find new owners through London's Battersea Dogs Home.

In a typical year the Battersea Dogs Home takes in around 10,000 unwanted or abused hounds. Each gets a full veterinary check-up, meals twice a day, a clean blanket daily, a home visitor to check out prospective new owners and one-to-one behavioural therapy (if needed). Thousands go on to find secure, loving homes. But, just occasionally, the loving gets too much.

Take the case of former Battersea resident Jasper, a Dobermann–Labrador cross rehomed with the brewery heiress, Diana Myburgh. When she died Jasper went to live with her former son-in-law, Sir Benjamin Slade, at his 13th-century manor house in North Newton, near Bridgwater, Somerset. The dog also inherited a nest egg administered by three legal advisers.

All went well until Sir Benjamin split with his girlfriend. She claimed Jasper was not being properly cared for and promptly whisked him off to her new London home. So began a tug-of-love battle unprecedented in the British judicial system.

'We went to court and Jasper paid all his own legal fees,' said Sir Benjamin. 'It became the only case in legal history where a dog has fought his own case. He won and later sued for £9,000.' In fact, while most mutts happily roll in fox and badger droppings, Jasper rolls in money. His fund manager has invested cannily on the stock market to turn the original legacy into a portfolio worth £130,000.

Not all dogs are quite so lucky. A student vet at San Simon University, Santa Cruz, Bolivia, was accused of killing his uncle's dog and boiling it in oil. He claimed his lecturers wanted animal skeletons and that students who brought in a dog were well rewarded. The idea of boiling the poor thing in oil was to remove its skin.

– AND WHO ARE YOU? –

Identity theft is increasing at an average rate of 3,000 per cent each year.

Anonymity is a thing of the past. Every time we use a credit card, surf the Internet, watch digital TV, or make a phone call some computer, somewhere, quietly ticks a box on its hard drive. This has spawned a new industry called 'data mining' in which companies (and the state) can piece together our private lives by trawling through disparate databases.

Keeping track of consumer buying habits via loyalty and credit cards gives the big chain stores a crucial marketing edge. Wal-Mart, the world's biggest retailer, now has the largest and most sophisticated commercial database in existence, a system capable of holding 200 terabytes – that's 200 million megabytes – of information, equivalent to 25 times the records and books held in the US Library of Congress.

Even if you don't view all this as an Orwellian nightmare, there are some big security issues at stake. Officials have a tendency to believe what computers tell them – ask anyone who's queried a tax bill – and that amounts to Bonus Round for fraudsters. It can't be a coincidence that the fastest-growing crime in America is identity theft.

– BERRY NICE –

Britons purchase an average of 110 tonnes of strawberries per day each summer.

Rain aside, few things symbolise a British summer quite like strawberries and cream. The figure listed above is set to rise with the arrival of the world's biggest commercial variety, the Spanish-grown Honor, measuring 63 x 76 mm (2.5 x 3 inches).

Inevitably, scientists have now produced a definitive formula for getting maximum taste from strawberries – just as well considering that tennis lovers pay around £8 per punnet at the Wimbledon championships. The secret is: perfect flavour = x grams strawberries + 0.5x grams cream. In other words, two parts strawberries to one part cream.

In fact, it's not quite as simple as that, according to Professor Andy Taylor, head of Nottingham University's Flavour and Food Department who carried out the research on behalf of Marks & Spencer. 'We've got a machine that measures aromas in the air and in food, and if you really want to sense the strawberry flavour then yoghurt is best for allowing the taste to come through,' he said. 'We're talking about plain, low-fat yoghurt. If you like cream then the more cream you put on, the more difficult it is to taste the strawberries.'

Somehow, strawberries-and-yoghurt doesn't have quite the same appeal. But then if we all listened to the Soil Association, sales would plummet by the punnet, whatever you plopped on. The organic campaign group says the typical strawberry receives 12 sprays a year to ward off insects and fungus and has among the highest levels of pesticide residue of all fruit and veg.

– PICTURE PERFECT –

Royal art treasures produce an average net income of £48,500 per week.

These are happy days for administrators of the Royal Collection, arguably the most important single collection of paintings anywhere in the world. The UK charitable trust in charge of the 565,000 items saw net income from exhibition admission charges and retail sales rise by around £30,000 per week – a dizzying 260 per cent – to £2.5 million in the year to 31 March 2003. And this in the year immediately following 9/11 when American visitors to Britain were about as commonplace as a Saddam Hussein look-alike at a Texan hog-roast.

Given that British royal palaces are stuffed with great historical works, it's perhaps understandable that the Queen and Duke of Edinburgh can be a bit sniffy about today's artists. Particularly where they themselves are the subject matter.

When in 2004 the Queen allowed herself to become the first royal hologram, a work commissioned by the island of Jersey to mark its 800th year of allegiance to the throne, she wasn't exactly effusive in her praise. After sitting through two 90-minute sessions with the artist Chris Levine, she was shown her three-dimensional image, painstakingly created from 10,000 digital photographs. 'It looks like an old woman lost in a wood,' she informed the camera crew.

Her irascible husband was still more forthright in his assessment of a partly-completed work by award-winning portrait painter Stuart Pearson Wright. This picture was always going to be a tad controversial, since it showed the Duke bare-chested with a bluebottle on one shoulder and four mustard seeds growing out of his right index finger.

The plants represent Charles, Andrew, Edward and Anne. The fly depicts mortality and consumption of decomposing human flesh. (Duh! Try to keep up.)

When the artist – known for his use of distortion or 'lengthenings' – allowed his subject a quick preview, the allegorical imagery rather left the duke cold. 'Gadzooks!' he exclaimed. 'Why have you given me a great schonk [a slang term for nose]?' Soon after this the Royal Society for the encouragement of Arts, Manufactures and Commerce (RSA), which had commissioned the work to celebrate Prince Philip's 50th anniversary as president, deemed it inappropriate. Mr Pearson Wright was packed off to produce a more traditional portrait.

It was hardly a shock rejection. Unveiling the original at a London gallery in April 2004, the artist recalled the prince's insistence that he wouldn't have it on the wall at Buck House. 'I asked him if he thought the face resembled his,' said Mr Pearson Wright. 'He replied: "I bloody well hope not."'

– STUDENT WOE –

Weekly rents for British students living in private halls of residence averaged £69.31 in 2002/03 – a 10.6 per cent rise in two years. Yet a survey by the National Union of Students shows the amount students can borrow to meet living costs rose by less than half over the same period, at 4.8 per cent. The NUS says that after paying a landlord, the average student starting a course in autumn 2004 had just £23.72 (£20.46 in London) per week to cover food, transport, books and clothes.

– JESUS SAVES THE STUDIOS –

In the USA, an average of 3,411,000 people per day bought cinema tickets in the first quarter of 2004.

Given the way Hollywood mucks about with history, it's ironic that the US film industry's saviour in 2004 was a movie about Jesus. Mel Gibson's *The Passion Of The Christ* took an average $3.5 million (£2 million) per day for the crucial winter quarter to 25 March, pushing US box office takings for the period to a record $21 million (£12 million) per day for all films. That translates to 290 million tickets, a 13 per cent rise on winter 2003. Without Gibson's efforts, the take would have been down 5 per cent.

Such was the clamour to see the film that it was rushed out a month early on DVD to deter pirating. The problem appeared particularly bad in Peru, where copyright experts believe just two in every 100 music CDs are genuine. The country's consumer protection agency confiscated everything from sophisticated copies downloaded from the Internet to shaky, hand-held video footage.

– MY FAVOURITE EAR –

Many items are said to be donkey's years old. But just how long does a donkey live? Actually, it is not the age of the donkey that's at the root of this common phrase but the length of his ears. The original phrase categorised items 'as long as a donkey's ears'. It seems that sometime during the First World War the words were merged – perhaps by someone with a West Country lilt – to become 'donkey's years'.

– RED TAPE TIGHTENS –

*Employment laws passed by the UK government
since 1997 have cost small and medium-sized companies an average £4.2 billion per year.*

Statistics like this one published by the British
Chamber of Commerce carry a double health
warning: 1. Company bosses don't usually flag
wave for the left-of-centre Labour Party (which
swept to power in 1997); 2. Employment laws get
in the way of making money. Still, the BCC insists
it has used the government's own figures to check
the cost of workplace compliance. Here's its
nattily-named 'Burdens Barometer': a top ten of the
red tape nightmares allegedly stifling British
business.

Law	Effect	Cost
Working Time Directive	Limits working week	11.20bn
Data Protection	Protects personal info	4.63bn
Pollution Directive	Cuts vehicle emissions	4.30bn
Asbestos Control	Monitors asbestos use	1.40bn
Disability Discrimination	Workplace equality	1.00bn
IR35	Requires Nat. Ins. on contractors' pay	973m
Employment Act	Family-friendly rights	565m
Working Tax Credit	Cuts for working parents	465m
Stakeholder Pensions	Makes firms offer pensions	404m
Flexible Working Rules	Gives right to flexible hrs	404m

The Top Ten Most Expensive Laws for UK Businesses

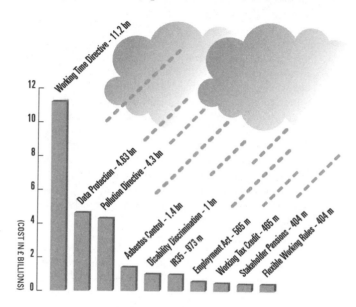

– NEXT ONE'S ON THE HOUSE –

Why can't all companies handle redundancy like brewers? In 2003 workers at a Guinness packaging plant in Dundalk agreed a severance deal offering free beer for ten years, as well as lump sum payments of up to £130,000. 'The beer allowance has been part and parcel of brewery life for a long time, not just in Guinness but around the world,' said spokesman Pat Barry. 'It works out at around two bottles a day.' Should keep those workers going until breakfast anyway.

– THE ROYAL SCAM –

Welfare fraud and error cost British taxpayers an average £2.7 million per day.

Few people – apart from asylum seekers, single mothers, Eurocrats and soccer thugs – enrage the British tabloids quite like a dole cheat. Stick your head out of the window next time one of these scumbag skivers hits the headlines and you'll be deafened by retired Colonels gnashing their teeth.

According to the Office for National Statistics, UK taxpayers lose £1.09 billion per year out of the total £117 billion welfare budget through fraud and claim errors. In 2003 11,000 people and 240 employers were prosecuted for benefit scams.

Funny thing, though. People who fiddle their tax returns don't seem to attract quite the same level of opprobrium. The government loses between £2 billion and £3 billion a year through tax evasion, yet the Inland Revenue carries out just 400 serious fraud investigations and 60 prosecutions a year among Britain's 30 million taxpayers.

Certainly, MPs are waking up to the problem. In January 2004 a report from the House of Commons public accounts committee pointed out that: 'To those involved in or contemplating [tax] fraud the chances of getting caught could appear minimal...the Revenue do not know how many people have tax haven bank accounts and credit card accounts...the major banks in this country...have not had to tell the Revenue about clients with an offshore account.'

Apart from which, fraud used to be so much more romantic. Take the case of Princess Caraboo from the island of Javasu in the East Indies. In April 1817 she was found wandering the streets of Almondsbury, Gloucestershire, apparently too proud to take a shilling from the parish's poor relief fund. She spoke no recognisable tongue.

The woman was taken to Knole Park, the gracious home of a local magistrate called Samuel Worrall and his wife Elizabeth. Elizabeth was intrigued by the way her strange guest went into raptures at a picture of a pineapple. She was determined to unravel the mystery and fortunately a visiting Portuguese sailor was able to understand the vagrant's language. He explained that she was a wealthy princess who had been kidnapped and sold to pirates for a bag of gold, later escaping to swim ashore to England.

The prospect of royalty in their midst produced a frenzy of activity in the Worrall household. The princess was painted by Thomas Barker, shown off to the local aristocracy and wined and dined the length of the county. Everything was fine until a Mrs Neale recognised the princess's description in the *Bath Chronicle* and realised that she was in fact Mary Baker, daughter of a cobbler from Witheridge, Devon, and former servant girl to the Neale family. Mary's party trick was to amuse the children by speaking an imaginary language. The 'Portuguese seaman' turned out to be neither Portuguese nor a seaman. As for Javasu, guess what...?

Despite this denouement, Mary packed herself off to America where her Caraboo scam continued in Philadelphia for several years. She later returned to penury and an anonymous grave.

– A FEATHER IN YOUR CAPEK –

The word 'robot' came into common usage via fiction rather than science. It was down to one Czech playwright whose name is hardly recognised today. Yet Karel Capek was a leading creator of science fiction stories just under a century ago and one of his most famous plays was about mechanised monsters rebelling against their master. The Czech word for mundane work was *robota,* so Capek named his characters robots. The word was first popularised in Czechoslovakia, then spread worldwide. A prize for science fiction writing that bears his name is still awarded annually in Prague.

– HIGH FLIER –

In the 2003–2004 season of England's Premiership, an average of 2.7 goals were scored in every match.

Football is something of an obsession among the Brits and there are many of you out there that won't need reminding that 380 matches were played in the Premiership last season, the country's soccer showcase. Of those, 44 per cent were home wins, 28 per cent were away wins and another 28 per cent were draws. The total number of goals scored was 1,012, of which 572 were scored at home and 440 were scored away. Top goal scorer was Thierry Henry, the fleet-footed French Arsenal striker who put away a total of 38 goals on behalf of his club: 30 in the Premiership, 3 in the FA Cup competition and 5 against European teams in the Champions League.

His goals were largely excellent, but none were as stunningly remarkable as the one attributed to 13-year-old Danny Worthington in 1999 in a match between his team, Stalybridge Celtic Colts, and Hollingworth Juniors in Manchester. Danny launched a strike on goal from a distance of 25 metres (82 feet), then turned away, convinced it was heading over the bar. And indeed it would have done so, had it not been for the intervention of a seagull that hove into view and literally headed the ball into the back of the net. The bird fell to earth, stunned by its heroic exertions. Happily, it quickly recovered and flew away, oblivious to the wonder and delight it had caused among the Stalybridge supporters. Referee Damian Whelan insisted the goal was good, claiming: 'If the ball does not go out of the pitch area, it can't be disallowed.' FA spokesman Steve Double backed the ref and added: 'To the best of my knowledge, a seagull has never scored a goal in football before.' Clearly luck was running against Hollingworth Juniors who eventually lost the match 7–1.

– FEAR OF FOREPLAY –

Sexual foreplay lasts for an average of 12 minutes.

Of course, being a victim of crime is never pleasant. But occasionally there are consolation prizes.

In the summer of 2001, Colombian police became aware of an innovative 'foreplay technique' used by three young female muggers. This involved dissolving powerful sedatives in water, rubbing the solution into their breasts, standing by the roadside in wealthy suburbs and inviting passing male motorists to stop for a lick. Those who took up the invitation quickly lost consciousness, along with their wallets and cars. When they came round they couldn't remember a thing.

It's not clear how much licking took place before the men fell into a stupor. However, the statistic listed above, published in the Canadian magazine *Urban Male*, can serve as a rough guide. Have you got the message yet, guys? Foreplay is DANGEROUS. Don't believe the advice columns. The women were later arrested in Bogota.

– BUSY ISLAND –

The population of Britain is expected to rise by an average 193,000 people per year, from 59.2 million in 2002 to 64.8 million in 2031, according to the Office for National Statistics. The UK government predicts that just over 50 per cent of this increase will be due to immigration; anti-migrant campaigners claim it will be closer to 85 per cent.

– ENGLISH CONQUERS EUROPE –

The expanded European Union turns out on average 46,000 pages of rules and directives, in 20 languages, every week.

Things are changing fast at the European Union, once regarded by London as a branch office of the French civil service. According to the Directorate of Justice and Home Affairs, more than 57 per cent of documents are now drafted in English, compared with 29 per cent in French and 5 per cent in German. Moreover, 69 per cent of Brussels job candidates from the ten new Eastern European countries chose English as their working language; just 14 per cent opted for French.

That said, the EU is still some way from adopting English as a Euro-wide standard for its 450 million citizens. The new member states have pushed the number of 'official' languages up from 11 to 20, providing jobs for 1,200 translators and 700 interpreters. This will increase the number of pages on rules and directives from the present average of 23,000 per week to 46,000. As for the interpreters, Brussels' target is to have 80 per language per day attending 11,000 meetings between them. The work can be tricky. A French linguist once translated the English word 'copyright' as 'a right to copy'.

No wonder the poor old EU is mercilessly vilified in Britain for its alleged love of bureaucracy. Fed up with the flack, Eurocrats are now striking back with an A-Z of top 'Euromyths' perpetrated by the media. The stories are said to be 'based on twisted facts or even lies'. Here's the best of them:

- Ambulances must be painted yellow
- Bananas and cucumbers mustn't be bendy
- Corgi dogs are banned
- Every egg to carry stamped details about the hen that laid it
- The euro causes skin disease and makes you impotent
- Tightrope walkers must wear hard hats
- The definition of an island has changed
- Model railways are under threat
- Noise will be banned in pubs and at football matches
- London's Waterloo Station to be renamed 'Europe Station'
- Playground swings are too high
- Employers must consult workers on factory tea brands
- Farmers will not be allowed to drive tractors
- Mountain climbers must use scaffolding
- Male EU staff are to get six free Viagra tablets per month

'The stories can make entertaining reading, but many people believe them and come away with a picture of the EU as a bunch of mad eurocrats,' says the website wistfully. Surely not.

– SHARP REMINDER –

Security guards confiscate 625 prohibited items every hour at Britain's airports.

There's a massive list of banned objects for air travellers, but that apparently doesn't stop passengers from kitting themselves up with worrying stuff before a trip. Every day security guards working for the British Airports Authority confiscate 15,000 items ranging from pen-knives to aerosols. Everything that can be recycled is recycled, so 90 per cent of metal objects and 80 per cent of things listed as 'hazardous products' will see another day with a new identity. BAA receives no financial benefit in the process.

– UP IN SMOKE –

About 15 billion cigarettes are sold across the world every day – which computes to about 10 million every minute.

It's a dangerous love affair in which mankind cannot find closure. The figures are, frankly, galling. At the moment, according to the World Health Organization, smoking kills one in ten adults globally and, unless present trends are overturned, that figure is going to increase to one in six by the year 2030. Every eight seconds someone somewhere in the world dies from an illness related to smoking. Research in the UK has proved that Cambridge, home of one of the nation's finest universities and presumably packed to the gunwales with hyper-intelligent types, is the smoking capital of Britain. Every year the average Cambridge household forks out £2,183 on tobacco – that's about 25 cigarettes a day. (Bracknell in Berkshire is the country's least smoky place, with just £183 spent annually in households on the equivalent of two cigarettes a day.)

A 50-year study among 35,000 male doctors into the long-term effects of smoking, published in the *British Medical Journal* in 2004, says that people who smoke will die ten years earlier than counterparts who do not. Among the doctors scrutinised, 81 per cent of non-smokers lived to the age of 70 compared with only 58 per cent of smokers. An estimated six million Britons died from the effects of smoking during the course of the study. One bright spot remains: that those who quit early enough can live as long as non-smokers.

Crucially, children are failing to get the anti-smoking message. Every day between 80,000 and 100,000 children worldwide begin smoking. The evidence is that about half of those who begin smoking in adolescence will smoke for at least a further 15 years. No one knows how to stop youngsters from smoking. If anyone did hit on a winning formula, they could bottle it and make a fortune from anxious parents.

But consider the following story that amply illustrates one barely highlighted folly of smoking. Two Ukranian soldiers sneaking a cigarette at work in an arsenal caused a £425 million fire that killed five people. The unnamed troopers sparked a blaze at the Melitopol warehouse complex where about 90,000 tonnes of munitions were stored. Flames ignited 5,000 explosions every hour and shells rained down on neighbouring villages and their terrified residents. Everyone in a 19-km (12-mile) radius of the complex had to be evacuated for several days until the fires had subsided. Defence minister Yevhen Marchuk observed: 'The armed forces are becoming a threat to their own people.'

– AMERICAN BEAUTY –

Across the globe, three Barbie® dolls are sold every second.

Bimbo or beauty? The argument rages on, but the long-term commercial success of the Barbie® doll is beyond doubt. Barbie® was the brainchild of Ruth Handler, one of the founders of Mattel Toys. She was inspired after watching her own daughter, Barbara, wrestle with the limitations of cardboard dolls with paper clothes. Barbie®, aka Barbie Millicent Roberts from Willows, Wisconsin, made her debut at the American Toy Fair held in New York in February 1959 with a $3 price tag and ascended to the heights of the toy hierarchy.

Her boyfriend Ken was created in 1961, and Barbie® has since had five sisters: Skipper (1964), Tutti (1966), Stacie (1992), Kelly (1995) and Krissy (1999).

She has also been given numerous different guises, including Army Barbie®, Olympic athlete Barbie®,

Presidential Barbie®, the best-selling Totally Hair
Barbie® and Friendship/Freundschafts Barbie®,
created to mark the levelling of the Berlin Wall.
Ken, too, has been given different identities. (My
own favourite is the Ken that winks when you press
a button on the back of his neck.)

Barbie® has had over 43 pets, among them 21
dogs, 14 horses, 3 ponies, 6 cats, a parrot, a chimp,
a panda and a zebra. More than one billion
fashions have been made for the multitude of
Barbies® brought into circulation since 1959 and,
staggeringly, if every mass-produced Barbie® was
placed head to toe with all her mass-produced
friends, the line they make would circle the Earth
more than seven times. Crikey.

However you feel about her, Barbie® cuts the
mustard in toy terms, achieving longevity in an
industry usually given to short-lived fads. Barbie®
has remained just about in the pink despite a recent
fall in worldwide sales. The disappointing results
posted in the first three months of 2004 were
thought to be the result of children casting around
for a new reality in toys.

Competitors these days tend to be grittier rather
than prettier – and they don't come much more
gritty than Death Row Marv. He is a 165-mm
(6.5-inch) tall plastic doll, based on a character in
the graphic comic *Sin City*. Strapped into a
battery-operated electric chair, his eyes glow red
when you flick the switch and, as he convulses, he
croaks: 'That the best you can do, you pansies?'
Definitely not one for the Christmas stocking
from Santa. It is unsurprising to discover that the
profile of buyers tends to be male, aged between
15 and 45.

(For anyone interested in the finer points, Marv is sentenced to death after the vengeful murder of the cannibalistic psychopath who killed a hooker named Goldie, the woman he loved. Nice.)

– HACKED OFF –

One in three home computers is infected with software capable of stealing account numbers, credit card details, secret passwords and other vital financial information.

Unlike computer viruses, the software or spyware gets to work without announcing its presence. It gets into machines on the back of seemingly innocent or unconnected downloads – with music lovers appearing to be the most at risk. While many act as advertisement prompts, a sizeable number are able to pass back relevant information to an unseen operator so they can use the pilfered numbers to pay for goods and services.

The extent of spyware activity was revealed in a survey called the Spy Audit, carried out upon 420,000 PCs by Internet service provider EarthLink and email company Webroot. It was discovered in no fewer than 143,000 machines, with the infected machines carrying an average of 28 spy programmes apiece.

Spyware is sometimes installed intentionally, in order that owners can track computer usage. But variants of it exist and are only evident by either an increase in the number of pop-up advertisements that appear on screen or a general go-slow in the computer functions.

Felicity Bull, of Britain's National Hi-Tech Crime Unit, said: 'This software can be used to steal your identity, including your bank details, and it is something we have seen a big increase in over the last few months.'

– WORKING TOO HARD? –

British workers clock up an average 41 hours per week.

In Europe statistics show that the UK, Germany and Austria are the most work-obsessed of the major states – with employees clocking up an average 41 hours per week. The Irish and Spanish deliver around 39 hours while the Finns, Danes and Belgians are well down the table at 38 hours. Most laid-back of all are the Italians, who manage just over 37 hours.

There are many that believe the Brits are on average working harder and longer than ever before. Not so, according to the government's Office for National Statistics, which maintains the national benchmark of 40 hours per working week has been the same for decades. It's the rural workers in Lincolnshire who are routinely clocking up more hours. The average working week there extends to 43.5 hours. Let's not forget that this is the home county of the mother of all hard workers, Margaret

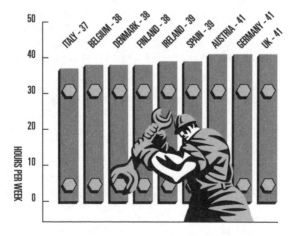

The Average Work Week in the European Union

Thatcher. She culled votes by broadcasting the dubious qualities of working 18 hours a day and sleeping only four hours a night, a paragon for the rest of us mere mortals. It didn't win her friends when it counted, though, did it?

We all like to think we are slaving away while the rest of the world looks on, even when we know full well that lengthy gossiping by the coffee machine and killer games of computer Solitaire shouldn't really be included as part of our working hours.

Yet the way we approach our 40 hours has perhaps changed. 'Work-life balance' is now *the* trendy phrase of Human Resources departments across the UK. About time when you consider these statistics from the Department of Trade and Industry:

• more than half the workforce suffers from stress, resulting in 6.5 million sick days a year;

• four million work more than 48 hours a week;

• one in 25 men works at least 60 hours a week;

• 350,000 more people are working a 48-hour week compared with a decade ago.

NB: Research from UK software development company WRQ shows that 10 per cent of employees work at least four hours a day outside their core hours. For employers this amounts to a 'buy two weeks, get one free' policy, according to WRQ. It amounts to £12,000 of free labour per employee per year. Is my editor reading this? *Is he?*

– LOAD OF RUBBISH –

Every American disposes of an average of 2 kg (4 lb, 8 oz) of garbage daily.

Rubbish is a constant problem – not the sort I talk, but the type that drifts about streets or beaches, overflows from the kitchen bin or is crammed into a landfill site to the rapturous delight of burgeoning colonies of seagulls and rats.

Refuse figures make unattractive reading. Every American is disposing of rubbish each day that's the equivalent in weight of two sugar bags, a massive hike on the figure of 50 years ago which stood at 1.4 kg (3 lbs, 2 oz), just a tad over a single sugar bag. Think about just how many Americans there are in 50 states and it gives you some idea about the problems here. In 2001 US residents, businesses and institutions chucked out more than 229 million tonnes of Municipal Solid Waste, only a limited proportion of which was recycled. According to the US Environmental Protection Agency, less than one-third is recycled or composted, while 15 per cent is burned and 56 per cent goes into landfill sites that are getting ever larger to cope with the demand.

Manufacturers are big rubbish producers and few are more acutely aware of the problems associated with waste disposal than toy giant Hasbro.

It was an early incarnation of this company that produced Flubber back in the early '60s, a name derived from two words: flying and rubber – and that probably tells parents all they need to know about this substance. Other adjectives can also be applied for those without the benefit of messy offspring, including blobby, stretchy, gooey and gunk.

Flubber has been the subject of no fewer than three movies. The first was made by Disney in 1961, called *The Absent Minded Professor* and starred Fred MacMurray and Nancy Olson. Such was its success, a sequel was made in 1963 called *Son Of Flubber* with the same cast. More than 30 years afterwards, the original was remade by Disney with Robin Williams.

Back in the '60s, toy makers spotted an opening in the market and filled it with Flubber, the sort of stuff that kiddies could manipulate to their hearts' content. It was launched in 1962 as being safe and non-toxic. But soon reports came back to the manufacturers thick and fast that children were coming up in blotches after playing with the product. Hastily reconvened testing boards discovered that Flubber had the potential to cause skin irritation in a percentage of the population. There was no option but to recall the tonnes of Flubber out there on safety grounds.

And that's when the problems really began. The company dispatched it to the local incinerator, but Flubber would not burn properly. As a large black cloud of Flubber fumes hung over the city, the remaining goo was sent back to Hasbro for disposal by a different means.

Company executives believed they had solved their dilemma by burial at sea. They duly got the relevant permissions and weighed it down on the sea-bed so nature could take its course. Alas, the Flubber wasn't ready to be sunk. The next day the company got a call from the Coastguard telling them that escaped Flubber was bobbing about on the ocean. Now the company had to foot the bills for an ocean-going clean-up operation – and still had to wrestle with the headache of how to get rid of it all when it was back on dry land.

Borrowing heavily from techniques honed by the Mafia, the last and most successful idea was to bury it under a building plot. Hasbro was constructing a new warehouse at the time and incorporated the rogue product beneath what was to become a parking lot. It seemed like the nightmare was over. However, even today Hasbro employees will tell you that on hot days Flubber oozes from between the car park cracks. The next film it features in will surely be a horror movie.

– GIVING IT THE RIGHT SPIN –

A Frisbee thrown at its optimum effectiveness will spin six times a second as it flies through the air.

Years of research by scientists have culminated in a fail-safe formula for Frisbee-throwers. Experiments carried out not just at one university but at many worldwide have deduced that successful Frisbee flight depends on the front being 10 degrees higher than the back at the point it is thrown. If the disc is flatter or more tilted when it takes off then it is likely to flip out in flight.

And it's the spin that keeps it stable, scientists have discovered. Fewer than six revolutions per second and the Frisbee is a goner. The lift is all down to the lip that gives it satisfactory stability. All of this investigation into a beach sport of dubious distinction seems a little over the top. Well, it would be if it were not for the fact that Frisbees and their flight paths have a whole heap in common with space probes. Scientists have been fitting gizmos to Frisbees to further the cause of space exploration. Writing in *New Scientist* magazine, planetary expert Ralph Lorenz, from Arizona University, explained: 'I can't deny that going out in the sunshine to test-fly a Frisbee is rather fun. But these tests do provide a cheap way of getting real flight measurements that can be used to refine the way signals from spacecraft are analysed.'

It's all a world away from the birth of the humble Frisbee, which took place at a Connecticut bakery in the 19th century, when employees began hurling aerodynamically-pleasing tin lids at one another.

– THICKER THAN WATER –

An average of 9,000 units of blood per day is needed in UK hospitals.

And although hospitals still struggle to fill this daily quota, the number of British blood donors remains a cause for national pride. The 2.5 million annual donations from 1.9 million people represent a greater proportion of willing givers among the population – 6 per cent – than other Western countries can muster. Only 5 per cent of the US population gives blood, while the figure in Australia, where one million donations are needed a year, is a lacklustre 3 per cent.

Obviously there are lots of fears about giving blood, not least that it will leave the donor an armful short. There have been plenty of different initiatives to counter this myth and highlight the importance of giving blood, the best probably coming from the Red Cross in Germany, where Count Dracula's only living relative volunteered to hammer the message home.

Ottomar Rodolphe Vlad Dracul, Prince Kretzulesco responded to a plea for blood donors. More than that, he agreed to emerge from a coffin to attract the interest of potential blood donors. Later he handed out autographs.

Prince Kretzulesco, who lives in a crumbling castle on the outskirts of Berlin, was adopted by Princess Katharina Olympia Caradja, a Romanian aristocrat and direct descendant of the notorious Transylvanian count.

Count Dracula, aka Vlad the Impaler, was known for feasting on the blood of his enemies during a 15th-century reign of terror. However, it was the vampire treatment he received from novelist Bram Stoker that really set his reputation alight. His story has spawned numerous films and ensured successful careers for the likes of Bela Lugosi and Christopher Lee.

– TALKING TURKEY –

No fewer than 91 per cent of Americans eat turkey at Thanksgiving.

Of the tens of millions of birds bought in the USA in that small window of time, about 24 per cent are bought fresh, while 69 per cent are bought frozen, according to the country's National Turkey Federation. As a meal, its popularity in America is such that turkey was the first meal Neil Armstrong and Buzz Aldrin ate on the moon. Abe Lincoln was more sentimental about this plump fowl that wandered in peace in the Americas ten million years ago, and refused to shoot them for food. He also saved the skin of his son's pet turkey called Jack. Benjamin Franklin had high hopes of the turkey becoming America's national emblem, although the somewhat superior-looking bald eagle won the day in the end.

Turkeys may be a lot of things, but they are not great fliers. Thus the annual Turkey Trot in the Ozark Mountains, Arkansas, has in the past attracted the attention of concerned anti-cruelty campaigners. The highlight of the Trot is the Turkey Drop, a dubious sport that involves turning 17 birds out of a low-flying plane over the town of Yellville, in the hope the creatures spread their wings and descend slowly into the streets. Despite the best intentions of the organisers, many of the birds are killed or injured in the stunt. (The year that birds with clipped wings were used was, frankly, disastrous.) The town fared little better when frozen turkeys attached to parachutes were used to save the live variety from the perils of flight. One destroyed the roof of a car while another smashed through a front porch.

Turkeys are sufficiently challenged in life without being tossed out of aircraft. For example, they can drown if they look up when it is raining. They can have heart attacks, too, as the US Air Force discovered when its planes broke the sound barrier above fields of turkeys, who promptly dropped dead from the shock.

At least the benighted turkey can thank its lucky stars it is not a passenger pigeon. In 1620 there were an estimated nine billion passenger pigeons in the small corner of America occupied by the Pilgrim Fathers. One man reported a flock 1.6 km wide and 386 km long (a mile wide and 240 miles long). Even 150 years later, a hunter could bring down 125 corpses with a single shot from a blunderbuss. Americans made such good use of the food stock that they were endangered by 1900. On 1 September 1914 the last passenger pigeon died of natural causes in Cincinnati Zoo.

– MAXED OUT –

About half of all Americans have a credit card with on-going debts, a Gallup Poll in 2004 revealed. Some 29 per cent of the population has at least one card but habitually clears the monthly bill. A fifth of Americans have no credit cards at all. If the outstanding balances on all American credit cards were spread among the entire US population – both card holders and non-card holders – the amount would add up to $2,947 per head.

– THE BIG SLEEP –

Statistics from the British government have revealed that every year doctors treat 96,000 people for sleep injuries. Indeed, the accidents that happen during slumber can be the most serious. Although there was only a one in two million chance of it happening, Danish fairytale writer Hans Christian Andersen died after falling out of bed.

– HAPLESS VILLAIN, BUMBLING THIEF –

Each year five million crimes are recorded in the UK, affecting on average almost one in ten of the population.

So much for violent crime. Now let's look at general felony which also haunts us. Fear of crime makes us turn our homes into fortresses and lock up our children. Yet as far as crime is concerned, we are not all average. The urban poor, single mothers and young men between the ages of 16 and 24 are genuinely at risk from wrong-doers. The middle classes and the elderly are least at risk.

But if only all the nation's villains were as incompetent as those listed below then we would sleep a lot more soundly in our beds.

A sneak thief could not resist the whisky bottle left in a public lavatory at the Royal Infirmary, Retford, while its owner made use of the facilities. Alas for the felon, the bottle belonged to a pregnant woman and rather than whisky it contained her urine, needed for tests at the maternity unit. 'I just hope whoever took it used a bit of soda water and ice to wash it down,' said the bemused loser.

A handbag snatcher fared little better when he mugged an 86-year-old woman out walking her dog in Netley Abbey, Southampton. He got away with the bag, to find it contained only the contents of her poop scoop.

Thieves could not resist the opportunity to place a bet on the horses using a recently stolen debit card. However, the card's rightful owner had the last laugh when the horse came in at great odds – and the winnings were paid into her account.

These bunglers have a great deal in common with the burglars of an Exmouth supermarket who stole £1,200 worth of electrical equipment, unaware it had all been returned by customers as faulty.

Police searching for a thief who stole a battery-operated Buzz Lightyear toy from a Hereford shop discovered their man hiding in bushes when the space ranger announced: 'Buzz Lightyear...permission to engage.'

A man posing as a policeman, who forced a car to stop in Brighton and began lecturing the driver, was swiftly arrested by the vehicle's occupants, who were all plain-clothes police officers.

Two cases of wine and two cases of a bottle called 'Silent Roar' were taken from a parked van in Coventry in 1997. While the name sounds like a fancy new cocktail, 'Silent Roar' is in fact lions' urine, used to keep cats off gardens. A police spokesman said: 'If they don't know what Silent Roar is, they might end up drinking the lot.'

Burglars who broke into a house in Essex during October 2000 found a pot labelled 'Charlie' and presumed it was cocaine for snorting. In fact, Charlie was the homeowner's deceased dog and the white powder was his cremated ashes. Police, who found the ashes arranged in neat lines, have no idea how much was ingested by villains before they made their getaway.

– YOU DO THE MATH –

Why does a baker's dozen amount to 13? In a bygone era, the law said loaves had to be a certain size. To avoid being prosecuted for underselling customers, bakers would add another loaf to a dozen to ensure there was legally enough yeast.

– SEX, LIES AND VIDEOTAPE –

It would take an average couple three and a half years to try each one of the 529 positions outlined in the Kama Sutra.

'Do you have sex often?' a therapist asks the heroine in the film *Annie Hall*.

'All the time, three times a week,' she replies.

When the same question is asked of her partner, played by Woody Allen, the answer is the same, only different. 'Hardly ever, three times a week.'

Here's the thing. The right and proper number of times to have sex in a week/month/year seems impossible to define.

Sex lives are strange and intangible. Humans and dolphins are the only animals to have sex for pleasure. And sometimes they join the rest of the world's species who consider it a chore. When it comes to sex, Brits can't even get their stories straight: one survey discovered that British men claimed to have sex twice a week while women who were asked confessed to once-weekly liaisons.

Yet there remains a fascination with sex and how it is done. The British Museum represents the national attitude towards sex in its insistence on keeping a collection of Victorian erotica firmly behind closed doors. Anyone keen enough to see the dusty old exhibits must apply in writing. Meanwhile over in Reykjavik, there's a refreshing Scandinavian-style openness with a Phallological Museum, housing the penises of more than 80 mammal species found in Iceland.

There's no rulebook to say that you're doing it right...unless, of course, you include the *Kama Sutra*, the Hindu spiritual guide to sex. It would take the average couple three and a half years to try each one of the 529 positions outlined in the book.

Then there's the sort of sex that goes on in isolation, usually involving a video machine, home computer, a telephone or perhaps a blow-up doll. The chief reason for their existence is that they're making truckloads of money for somebody, somewhere.

According to Naughty Linx, an online index maintained by JMR Creations of Boston, the Web boasts some 28,000 sex sites, about half of which are set up to make money. The only problem with this figure is that it was out of date before it was even announced. New sites are opening all the time, giving customers greater choice than ever before.

The New York-based market research firm Media Metrix reports that 30 per cent of American households with Internet access visit an adult site at least once a month – but that only accounts for those prepared to admit to it.

Indeed, the income generated by sex films, for example, is almost impossible to estimate, since few release figures and most industry analysts pretend they don't exist. A rare exception is Forrester Research of Cambridge, Massachusetts, which has gone so far as to venture that sex sites on the Internet account for at least 10 per cent of Web-based retail in the USA. That's heaps of dosh and rising.

– MUGGER'S GAME –

Violent crimes recorded by police have risen to an average of 2,465 per day in England and Wales.

Every politician knows that crime figures play big with the voters come election time. Trouble is, interpreting the statistics really does your head in.

Take the figures for violent crime – which includes murder, rape, robbery and muggings – in England and Wales. Home Office statistics show that offences recorded by police have risen from around 600,000 (average 1,643 per day) in 1998 to 900,000 (average 2,465 per day) in 2003. That's a massive 50 per cent hike...and yet the British Crime Survey, which canvasses the public's *actual* experiences, suggests that violent crime has *fallen* since 1995 and now remains 'stable'. One explanation is that the police have got better at recording crimes. So that's all right then.

In America the Justice Bureau's statisticians do things slightly differently, working out what's known as the AVR or 'adjusted victimization rate'. This shows that the number of violent crime victims aged 12 or over has fallen from an average of 5 per 1,000 in 1978 to barely 2 per 1,000 in 2002 – the lowest level ever logged.

It all sounds vaguely comforting, although bear in mind the postcode (zip code) lottery effect that applies to both countries. For instance British Home Office figures show that two-thirds of all robberies take place in police areas containing just 22 per cent of the total population.

Unfortunately there are no official figures for 'muggers getting their come-uppance' which, let's face it, would be far more fun to wade through. But in the interests of public morale, *The Lore of Averages* brings you these anecdotes to truly warm the heart.

Quick-thinking staff at Burger King in Ypsilanti, Michigan, told an early morning raider that they could not open the cash register without a food order. The gun-wielding robber obediently placed an order for onion rings, only to be told that they were not available at breakfast time. Frustrated, the man walked away empty-handed.

A burglar from Indiana left his false teeth at the scene of his crime after they fell out of his mouth when he tripped. The gnashers, which bore his name on the artificial gum, informed police about the identity of the villain.

The following story also provides clear proof that there is a God and that He doesn't like his people messed with. How else can you explain the fate of 40-year-old Edward Sanders, who moseyed up to a Salvation Army worker in Tucson, Arizona, in December 2003 and snatched her collecting tin containing $70. Minutes later he was knocked down by a Honda car, arrested and banged up in Pima County Jail. As Sergeant Dan Snyder put it: 'God has a poetic sense of justice.'

– BITTERSWEET PARTNERSHIP –

Why are M&Ms called M&Ms? The name is from the initials of the founding fathers of this confectionery business, Forrest Mars and Bruce Murray. Mars was the son of the founder of the confectionery company, while Murray was a member of the clan that made Hershey bars. By rights they should have been bitter rivals. In fact, they teamed up primarily for sound business reasons, in order that Forrest could get sufficient amounts of chocolate for his sweet idea while Murray could get a bite at a new business. The candy-coated sweets first appeared in the USA in 1941 and were a swift success with American troops as the chocolate didn't melt in their hands. In the UK they were known as Treats until a name change in 1987.

– DIVORCING REALITY –

One divorce takes place in Britain every three minutes.

The number of divorces registered in the UK in 2002 was 160,700, a rise of almost 4,000 on the previous year. It means that 3,090 occur each week; that's more than 440 a day, 18 an hour and one in just a tad over three minutes. The average age of divorce among men is 41.3 years, while in women it is 38.8 years. Meanwhile the number of marriages taking place annually has come down to 291,800.

It's depressing reading, yet some folks are still desperate to get hitched. To assess their chances, it helps to know that for every 100 married people in the UK there are 90 who are single. Conversely, for every 100 unmarried people there are 111 already wed.

Britain has the highest divorce rate in Europe. Although it is equalled by Finland, it far outstrips that of Italy, which boasts the lowest rate. And because of that, the solicitors' firms are keen to capitalise on marital misery. One London law firm was deemed to have overstepped the mark, though, when it produced a poster campaign with slogans such as 'Ditch the Bitch' and 'All Men Are Bastards'. The posters were placed strategically in the rest rooms of upmarket London bars.

The slogans reflect the passions that divorce can arouse, so aptly portrayed in the 1989 film *The War Of The Roses*, starring Michael Douglas and Kathleen Turner. In the movie the couple are so embittered that they wreck their home in a bid to destroy one another. And that's just about what happened to a British couple in 2004 who spent more than 40 per cent of their combined fortunes on legal bills as each tried to wring more concessions out of the other. The divorce proceedings began in 1998 after ten years of marriage, when the couple was thought to be worth something in the order of £1.2 million. Six years later, the legal bills had amounted to £570,000 – and would have risen further without the intervention of an Appeal Court judge who kicked out a last ditch attempt to revise the divorce agreement.

Mrs Justice Baron decided at the High Court three months earlier that the wife should receive 57 per cent of marital assets and the husband 43 per cent. She commented: 'It would seem that the parties have used between 40–50 per cent of their worldly worth in pursuit of the issues in this case.' The pair has remained unnamed to protect the identity of their teenage son. (You can't help but feel sorry for the little guy, whoever he is.)

The rising divorce rate puts Britain in the same league as America, where between 43 and 50 per cent of marriages end in divorce. One in three marriages ends within the first ten years. And some come to a finish before that, as the statistics attached to Glynn Wolfe reveal. Wolfe had been married 29 times before his death in 1997, aged 88, at San Bernardino in California. He was approaching his first anniversary with his last wife, herself a veteran of numerous weddings.

– PLEASE SHOOT ME –

Easy to imagine that the phrase 'son of a gun' translates to offspring of a happy-go-lucky kind of dad – and in a way it does. It harks back to a time when women were allowed to visit and even live on naval ships. Unsurprisingly, a great number became pregnant and bore their child aboard, usually in the vicinity of the midship gun, and only sometimes with the benefit of a material screen. If the identity of the father was unknown – as was often the case – the baby was recorded in the ship's log as the son of a (midships) gun.

Another naval term that has become part of everyday parlance is 'square meal', so-called because sailors ate from square or rectangular wooden boards. And when people are 'three sheets to the wind' it is because they have the rolling gait of a ship that's lost control of its sails to the wind. 'Knowing the ropes' is another nautical expression that came into being when rigged ships had literally miles of lines to keep the sails in place. A ship's sail also spawned the phrase 'footloose'. The bottom of a sail is known as its foot. When it is unsecured it pretty well does as it pleases in the wind, thus the term footloose came into common parlance.

In days gone by, the deck was known as the board. Anything on deck in full view was 'above board' while items in the sea floating past had 'gone by the board'.

The original 'slush funds' were created in the British navy. When ships came into port, the cook would scrape together the fatty remains in the meat storage barrels, gathering a slurry known as slush. He sold it ashore and the proceeds, generally shared among the crew, were known as slush funds. Now we've come to the bitter end of naval phrases, that is, the end of the anchor cable which was fastened to the bitts at the ship's bow. When all the anchor cable was used up it was known as 'the bitter end'.

– CHEERLESS –

The average family spends £14.80 a week on alcohol, compared with £3 a week on children's clothes.

Enjoying a drink is one thing. But the way many thousands of British men and women consume alcohol is quite another. They binge on it, ending short periods of abstinence with sustained and heavy drinking bouts. Adults who like a tipple too much are a mighty drain on the country's resources. Government figures reveal that more than a third of those who attend hospital casualty departments go as a result of drinking excessively. (They could have become ill through drinking or been injured by someone who was drinking.) The nation's boozers cost the National Health Service something between £1.6 and £1.7 billion a year.

It is estimated that a million children are directly affected by the drinking habits of their parents and copious drinking seems to be a lesson we adults can quickly impart to the young.

Consequently, nine children a day are admitted into hospital in England after binge drinking.

According to figures from the Department of Health, 3,322 children aged between 11 and 15 went to hospital in a single year for treatment after drinking alcohol. Of those, 562 suffered from toxic poisoning. A fanfare of warning has also been sounded by the Salvation Army, which carried out a survey in 2003 to discover that alcohol consumption among teenagers has doubled in the past decade.

It's not just a British thing. The World Health Organization believes that alcohol is responsible for more than 9 per cent of Europe's disease tally. That's less than our old friend tobacco, but much, much more than illegal drugs, thought to cause less than 2 per cent of the continent's serious illness. One in four deaths among European men aged between 15 and 29 is alcohol-related.

– BED HEADS –

The average person sleeps for about 220,000 hours during a life-time – which amounts to 25 years.

That figure is astonishing, given everything that stands in the way of some solid snoozing.

The worldwide rate of insomnia is difficult to gauge, although those who eat and drink late, women in middle age, night workers and those in stressful jobs seem unduly affected. Then there's restless legs syndrome, a condition that gives sufferers a twitching, burning sensation in their limbs that can only be alleviated by walking around. Recent research carried out by Dr Wayne Hening in New York revealed that about one million Britons were afflicted. It particularly affects people when they are at rest in bed.

For many, overcrowding is a problem. When an adult sleeps with a partner in an average sized double bed – say, 1.3 metres wide by 1.8 metres long (4' 6" wide and 6' 2" long) – he has less personal space available to him than a baby in a cot.

But maybe a bit of sleeplessness is a good thing. Research published by the London Sleep Centre revealed that one study into longevity discovered the best survival was among those who sleep between 6.5 and 7.5 hours on weekdays.

Moreover, the mortality risk of those sleeping more than 7.5 hours nightly is a bigger worry than the risk of those who sleep less than 6.5 hours. Only those who reported less than 4.5 hours of sleep a night experienced significantly increased mortality. The results debunked the widely-circulated hypothesis that it is best to sleep at least 8 hours.

This isn't good news for narcoleptics, those people who fall asleep at inappropriate moments, generally against their will. There's a long-standing joke about the problems facing the narcolepsy support groups that exist, namely that no one stays awake long enough to take the minutes. In fact, only two people out of every 10,000 in America will suffer from the debilitating illness. (Bizarrely, the figure rises to 16 people out of every 10,000 in Japan.)

Staying awake can be the hardest task in all the world, even for those without narcolepsy – even when our lives and others depend upon it.

In a letter to the *Sunday Telegraph*, former pilot David Harlow confided his method of making sure someone was always awake on the flight deck. 'Just before take-off I would squeeze the First Officer's thigh. If he liked it – I didn't sleep. If he didn't like it – he didn't sleep.'

– BARE FACED CHEEK –

An average sneeze can spread up to 10 million germs, at speeds of up to 160 kilometres per hour (103 mph).

In fact, the swift infection rates of illness through coughs, sneezes and bodily fluids has brought the surgical mask into vogue. Those who worked with the sick and those who were fearful of being afflicted donned a mask every time they stepped outside until they became must-have items. Few construed the masks as anything more than a common-sense precaution.

Yet fetishes come in all shapes and sizes, and sometimes those deep-rooted desires can get you into hot water. And so it was with 53-year-old Norman Hutchins, who in June 2004 was banned from all British hospitals, GP surgeries and dental surgeries following a concerted campaign to acquire surgical masks. Hutchins was made the subject of an anti-social behaviour order after York magistrates heard he had made 47 attempts to obtain surgical garments by deception in five months. Hutchins claimed he needed the masks for amateur dramatic productions.

Presumably he was subject to similar urges as a 55-year-old Japanese man who was arrested three months earlier for stealing women's underwear. Police raided his home to find 4,000 pairs of knickers, collected over 30 years. The knicker nicker was nicked as he climbed on to a balcony to increase his haul and was discovered by the husband of one of his victims. 'I love women's underwear and could not control my desire,' the man told a television network.

He is not alone. In 1998 a Danish man with similar inclinations spent hours fishing bras and pants off the rails of a top-notch lingerie store through the shop's letterbox. Police were perplexed by the crime. 'Of course we're looking into this,' said a spokesman. 'But honestly, we don't really know where to look.'

– AND THE WINNER IS... –

Since the Swedish supergroup Abba first made the pop charts in 1974, it has sold an average of 13,333,333 records and CDs every year.

Once upon a time, not so long ago, it was impossible to mention the words 'Eurovision Song Contest' without smirking. There's something about the somewhat kitsch competition that brought out the bitch in all of us and it was mercilessly lampooned for producing poor-quality pop.

Well, perhaps we could have done better than Britain's 2003 entry 'Cry Baby' by Jemini that famously attracted nil points. But there have been some belters to emerge from the ranks of the mundane, including records by Celine Dion, Dana, Johnny Logan, Katrina and the Waves, Nana Mouskouri, Lulu and more.

Today there's a revival of interest in the televised singing competition, with people openly admitting to watching and enjoying it when before it was very much a closet thing.

The Eurovision Song Contest certainly brought an enduring smile to the lips of the two couples that comprised the group Abba, lasting from 1974 when they won the contest with 'Waterloo' until the present day.

Like the show, Benny, Bjorn, Agnetha and Frida pulled in the audiences but committed the cardinal sin of being 'uncool'. They too have undergone a makeover that has left them at the peak of chic more than 20 years after cutting their final disc together.

Abbamania has been ably assisted by two Australian films featuring Abba tracks: *The Adventures Of Priscilla, Queen Of The Desert* and *Muriel's Wedding*; by long-lasting West End musical *Mamma Mia,* featuring the group's music; not to mention popular tribute acts like Björn Again. Today there's hardly a corner left on Earth that hasn't been entertained by the sounds of 'Dancing Queen' or 'Take A Chance On Me'.

Recently Björn himself admitted: 'A friend was recently in the African bush on safari. He was enjoying the sun, the great silence of the plains, when suddenly he heard the sound of "Dancing Queen".'

Despite their continued popularity, the group has never once reformed for a revival concert since splitting in 1981.

– SWEET TOOTH WITH BITE –

Americans eat about 275 million pounds of honey each year.

The US taste for honey keeps untold millions of bees busy with its production. However, making honey and other beehive items is no longer the genteel industry it once was. That's because of the introduction of killer bees, which are not the product of a Hollywood B movie director's fervid imagination, but really exist.

Just ask the 77-year-old Las Vegas woman who was lucky to escape with her life after being swarmed by killer bees. Two police officers who tried to rescue her were also stung, and eventually firefighters were called in to douse the last 200 of the insect marauders. According to Associated Press reports filed in March 2000, the head of Beemaster Pest Control, Rodney Behring, who was given the task of tracking the bees down and destroying them, discovered the hive in a hollow tree with an estimated 40,000 bees in residence. Science says that more than 50 per cent will get involved in an attack, which means the unfortunate victim was buzzed by some 20,000 of them. She was in a critical condition after being stung about 500 times.

Killer bees are the colloquial name for Africanized Honey Bees, similar in appearance to their European cousins but considerably more aggressive. They were taken from Africa to Brazil in 1956 by scientists trying to create a busier-than-ever hybrid bee. Alas, some escaped and, after intermingling with regular bees, spread across the Americas. Their sting is no worse than normal bees, but they attack in greater numbers.

These are bees with severe attitude that swarm at the drop of a hat. Estimates vary wildly, but the worst case scenario is that they have claimed 1,000 lives since their inadvertent introduction. In December 1999 four-year-old Kharin Toloza was playing with his dog at his home in Argentina. Lucky Kharin survived because the dog jumped on top of him. Sadly, the hero dog died.

Having created the menace, scientists are keen to find the silver lining to this dark cloud. In 2002 it was announced with some satisfied triumph that killer bees were terrific news for the coffee harvest. The pollination they provided appeared to increase yields by up to 50 per cent. Relief all round then, if the only buzz you are getting is the one that comes in a cup.

– EGYPTIAN CURSE –

The frustrating experience of waiting alone in front of an empty luggage carousel in a deserted baggage hall after a long and exhausting flight is not uncommon. According to a survey carried out by the Churchill Insurance Company in 2000, no less than 11 per cent of airline travellers in the UK finished a trip minus their bags. Curiously, the place that lost luggage was most likely to turn up again was Cairo.

– JAVA SPEAK –

Americans drink about three and a half cups of coffee per head per day.

Only in the USA could you order a double tall, half caff, low fat, no foam, extra hot, non-whip mocha latte – and have a small chance of someone knowing what you were talking about. Americans crave their cappucinos, espressos are irresistible to them and an astonishing 500 million cups are daily swallowed stateside. That makes for about two and a half billion pounds of the stuff consumed each year – about one-fifth of the world's coffee harvest.

In the UK, it's an all-round quicker experience. It's hard to walk down the high street without becoming hyperactive from airborne caffeine particles generated by fresh-brew coffee shops – which is surprising since 44 per cent of Brits drink *only* instant coffee. This compares to 6 per cent of Germans, 11 per cent of the French and 18 per cent of the Spanish. The consumer analyst Mintel concludes that Brits have too hectic a lifestyle to bother with proper coffee.

As a result of its popularity it has been linked to all manner of diseases, but the medical evidence about allegedly harmful effects is doubtful. The one arena where it does appear to be detrimental to health is in the case of pregnant women and those trying for a baby. (Consult your doctor for further information.)

The one issue that continues to exercise coffee drinkers is whether or not it is addictive. Well, no one has yet been found to have mugged old ladies or stolen out of their parents' wallets to finance a coffee habit. Few if any people have been reduced to sleeping in cardboard boxes after getting hooked. There are no recorded incidents of people being found insensible on street corners in the early hours after consuming too much coffee.

But yes, its caffeine content does keep coffee drinkers coming back for more. Caffeine is a mild stimulant of the central nervous system that makes us feel more focused. A cup of brewed coffee contains more than instant coffee and has about two and a half times more caffeine than the equivalent cup of tea. Coffee contains about five times more caffeine than cola drinks.

However, before you turn your back on Starbucks forever, consider also the caffeine content of other items. Caffeine crops up in cold remedies and diet pills. If you had a caffeinated pain reliever, then you consume almost half the amount of stimulant that you would in a cup of freshly brewed coffee – without having the benefit of the to-die-for aroma. Pop a diet pill and that's virtually the caffeine equivalent of a cup and a half of coffee going down.

– DOUBLING UP –

About 15 in every 1,000 UK births result in twins, triplets or more.

The number of twin or multiple births is on the rise. Take Norway as an example. Recent reports reveal that twice as many twins were born there in 1999 as were born in 1986. For the record, in that year it notched up 1,031 sets of twins, 21 sets of triplets and a single set of quadruplets.

Likewise Britain has more twins than ever before. On average, 15 in every 1,000 births result in twins, triplets or more, an increase of 20 per cent in 10 years. And that's only half the rate that America enjoys.

During 2000 there were 118,916 twin births in the States, as well as 6,742 triplet births, 506 sets of quadruplets and an astonishing 77 quintuplets plus coming into the world. That's a 74 per cent increase in the number of twin births since 1980. So for American women the chances of having a multiple birth are about 3 per cent.

Of course, the double baby boom is largely down to improved fertility treatments, although more women are staving off family life until they reach their 30s, when the chances of having a multiple birth increase. The number of identical twins who have come from the same, shared fertilized egg has remained steady. It is the number of fraternal twins, the product of two eggs in the womb, that has forged forward.

There are lots of dilemmas that accompany the arrival of twins. Should they be dressed the same or differently? Will they communicate telepathically? Will one be an evil twin?

The parents of Johnny and Luther Htoo possibly pondered in all seriousness those three points when they looked at their young twins. The boys with pea-pod likeness were chain-smoking, gun-toting rebel guerillas clad in fatigues before they reached their teens. Living in a remote mountain area, they fought for independence for the Karen minority from the ruling Burmese as part of God's Army (so-called because they lived on God's mountain). The lads and fellow army members were a bit Christian, a bit Buddhist and a lot into the local folk religion. Consequently, the youngsters were quickly imbued with magical powers.

They were believed to be immune from bullets, possess the power of invisibility and the ability to call up 5,000 spirit soldiers, always an asset when you are outnumbered by the military. At least some of this notoriety was rooted in extraordinary exploits witnessed in battle. Both had black tongues.

Ultimately, aged just 13, the boys grew weary of a life of emotional and physical deprivation. They gave themselves up to neighbouring Thailand and resigned themselves to a life less glamorous in a refugee camp. Some Karen hardliners still cling to the hope that they will return to vanquish their foes.

– LOVE FROM THE HEART –

Heart-attack victims with someone to love halve their risk of suffering a repeat attack, according to a study of 600 patients by doctors at Manchester Royal Infirmary. One theory is that people who enjoy a close relationship with a lover, friend or relative have lower levels of the stress hormone cortisol – linked to weak immune systems and high blood pressure.

Almost three-quarters of the patients, who had an average age of 60, were men. Those without a close relationship were more likely to drink, use illegal drugs and have suffered a previous heart attack. They were also twice as likely to have been separated from their parents during childhood – a factor which may, say researchers, have exposed them to high levels of cortisol early in life.

– MAY BE LUCKY –

Are you an optimistic, relentlessly positive person? Or a right old grumpy gills who thinks the world is against you? Whichever, scientists believe it may not be your fault. Research by Professor Richard Wiseman of the University of Hertfordshire suggests a correlation between the time of year you were born and the breaks you reckon come your way. His survey of 40,000 people concludes that May babies are most likely to believe they are born lucky while October-borns tend towards the opposite view.

'It is quite a significant finding and there is some good evidence that people born in the summer are a bit more optimistic and resilient,' said Professor Wiseman. 'It could be to do with the effects of temperature on birth or parental styles. For instance, parents may be more optimistic and happy in the summer, which may rub off on the child. The good news for winter-borns is that people can improve their luck by being more optimistic and making the most of the opportunities that come their way.'

We can assume that retired teacher David Harrison was born in the depths of winter. Accidents happen, but you'd rightly consider yourself unlucky if a vehicle smacked into the side of your house causing catastrophic damage. Well, that bizarre domestic disaster has happened to Harrison not once, not twice but three times in just seven years. In the spring of 2004 his home in Powburn, Northumberland, was wrecked when a 44-tonne truck ploughed into the living room. 'If I'd been downstairs I would have been killed,' he said afterwards. The accident happened while David was awaiting repairs for the damage caused by a runaway car earlier the same year. Seven years ago a lorry caused £13,000 worth of rebuilding work.

Scarborough goalkeeper Leigh Walker is surely another winter baby. He had a similar sinking sensation when his mum washed a keepsake Chelsea shirt, autographed by the premiership team. Walker was presented with the shirt by his opposite number Carlo Cudicini, after Chelsea defeated his team in a fourth round FA Cup. On it Cudicini wrote: 'To Leigh, all the best for the season.'

Walker said: 'I'm gutted. It was a special souvenir of the biggest match I've ever played. Now it's ruined.'

His mum explained: 'I saw the writing and didn't intend getting rid of it. I thought I could wash the sleeves without touching the rest of the shirt, but the water spread and washed off all the writing.'

Rock fan Tim Walker, however, must have been born on the cusp of spring. He believed the £1,000 he invested at a charity auction in a guitar bearing the signature of Queen guitarist Brian May was money well spent. He changed his tune, though, after playing a favourite Oasis track on the instrument – and wiping off the moniker with his sleeve. His bad luck ended when May – and who knows if the name is significant here – offered to repeat the inscription at no extra charge.

– SEEING THINGS –

On average the human brain can only remember four things at one time.

Ever wondered about your brain's visual short-term memory capacity? Possibly not, but as an exercise in humbling the human race, studies on VSTM are proving good value.

The sad truth is that a penny-sized piece of our brains known as the posterior parietal cortex is responsible for remembering objects or details encountered in a particular scene. On average, humans can remember just four things – a truly woeful statistic suggesting that this bit of grey matter has evolved hardly at all since our Stone Age ancestors invented hot food by rubbing sticks together.

To prove the point, Dr Daniel Simons of the University of Illinois and Dr Daniel Levin of Vanderbilt University, briefed a researcher to stop students inside a college campus and pretend to be lost. During these conversations two accomplices walked between researcher and student carrying a large door. This allowed the first researcher to be substituted for another of different height, build and appearance. Despite the fact that they had spoken to the lost stranger for 10–15 seconds, half the students didn't notice that they'd ended up chatting to a different person. They had been unable to absorb enough detail – a phenomenon known as 'change blindness'.

It gets better. VSTM was put to the test in another scenario devised by Simons and a Harvard University colleague, Christopher Chabris. They asked their subjects to watch a videotape of a few people playing basketball. The task was to count the number of passes made by one of the teams.

At the end of the experiment – considered a classic by US academics – subjects were asked if they had spotted anything unusual occur during the film. Around half said no, nothing else happened. Did they not then notice the woman dressed in a gorilla suit who walked slowly across the scene for nine seconds, passing between the players and turning to the camera to thump her chest? Apparently not.

Some of the subjects later refused to accept that the gorilla had made an appearance and insisted that the re-run tape was an edited version. When the tape was played to other subjects, without any specific instructions, they all saw the gorilla lady.

Apart from an insight into the inadequacies of the human brain, these findings surely have big implications for sports coaches. How many times do you hear players accused of 'ball watching' when they should be checking the movement of those around them! Maybe college jocks need to invest in gorilla outfits to become totally invisible during matches. Unless, of course, they're already gorillas posing as jocks.

– TICKETS TO RIDE –

Every six minutes a driver is caught speeding in Britain.

Death and taxes are supposed to be the only two certainties in life, but if you're a UK motorist you can now add speeding fines to the list. Home Office figures show that between 1996 and 2002 the number of drivers caught by speed cameras rose five-fold from 262,200 to 1,411,300. In other words, someone now gets busted once every six minutes. Together these drivers have handed government bureaucracies a £90 million windfall from fines.

It gets worse. Under the totting-up system, by which motorists receive penalty points for traffic offences, 30,500 people lost their licences in 2002 – many of them tipped over the 12-point trigger limit by snap-happy traffic cops. A further 184,000 people were disqualified for specific offences, a year-on-year rise of 18,500.

As if to enter into the spirit of things, police and traffic wardens issued a combined total of 3.1 million penalty notices and on-the-spot fines in 2002 (an annual increase of 4 per cent) while local authority parking attendants dispensed further misery with a confetti-like distribution of parking tickets – 6.1 million (a 21 per cent increase). In fact, the only drivers with cause to celebrate are the crap and drunk ones. Breath tests on suspected drink-drivers were down 9 per cent while careless driving offences fell by 8 per cent.

The problem with speeding and parking fines is that they tend to be random. For example, are the residents of Essex accelerator addicts and speed freaks? That's what recently released government figures would have us believe, as no fewer than 213,861 drivers were fined for speeding in the county in 2002–2003. That's 50,000 more than any other county in England and Wales and represents one in six of the county's population. It also generated a mighty £13 million for the local police and council.

Compare the figures with some other counties in the league table of speeding fines. Only 6,665 drivers were fined for speeding on the open roads of North Yorkshire, 5,205 were caught in Gwent while just 4,799 were nabbed in Gloucestershire.

Beleaguered Essex drivers claim their driving habits are no worse than anywhere else, but they are more likely to get caught thanks to 90 speed cameras at roadside locations monitoring their movements. Mounting a fightback against what they believe is police harassment, angry drivers began visiting a website that publicises the current whereabouts of the mobile cameras in Essex.

There have been occasional reports of vandalism against speed cameras, but no British driver has yet been pushed so far over the edge that he or she lives out a secret traffic-cop fantasy. Unlike James Winton.

In 2003 Winton, a 41-year-old from Barrie, Canada, was pretending to be a cop on a county road near New Lowell when a car carrying two guys overtook him. Winton immediately switched on the flashing red lights fixed to his white Neon and impatiently signalled for them to pull over. Wearing *de rigeur* police sunglasses, he then strutted over to deliver a lecture on the speed limit and the stupidity of those who abused it. Unfortunately, the man emerging from the passenger door was off-duty policeman Constable Jarrod Hunter.

Hunter had seen the flashing red lights from some way off and immediately clocked that something was wrong. He'd asked his father-in-law to deliberately pass the Neon; now he could put his suspicions to the test. Before the would-be cop could wag a finger, Hunter demanded: 'Let me see your tin.' This brought a blank look so Hunter whipped out his authentic police badge and slapped it on the car bonnet. 'Your badge,' he explained meaningfully, 'I want to see one of these.'

Winton claimed he'd forgotten it, but insisted he was a legitimate officer for Peel Region. By way of response, Hunter leant inside the Neon, jerked the keys out of the ignition and called his colleagues. Inside the Neon's boot they found several fake police jackets, a pamphlet on criminal law, a holster, several hundred rounds of ammunition and a semi-automatic gun. Winton, who pleaded guilty to impersonating a police officer, got six months' jail, two years' probation and a court recommendation for psychiatric counselling.

– TIS THE SEASONING –

It's a compliment to say someone is worth their salt – even when salt costs next to nothing these days and is something of a bad guy because of its associations with hypertension. Of course, the phrase came into being centuries ago when salt was far more precious than it is today and its health implications were unknown. Jesus told his disciples they were the 'salt of the earth'. There's evidence that Roman soldiers were even partly paid in salt, hence the word 'salary'.

– MASSAGE MAIL –

On average, UK employees spend nearly 49 minutes a day managing their email but just 25 minutes a day playing with their children.

How sad is that? Yet despite enslaving ourselves to the Great God Outlook Express it still kicks us in the teeth. Just ask Sharon Dyson, whose missive to her boyfriend about a Sunday afternoon shopping trip, some sexual banter and a snipe at clients dumped her in big trouble.

Dyson, a student careers adviser, told London PR executive Alex Hewson: 'My sunburn on my back is sore and I need you to rub some moisturiser in for me.' She went on in none-too veiled terms about massage oil, sucking up to clients and personal stress-busting techniques that need no further explanation on these pages.

Oh dear. Dyson accidentally clicked the 'reply all' icon on an email she'd received earlier from Hewson. This instantly transmitted her words to 30 of his friends who gleefully forwarded it to their mates. Within hours it was all over the City and, inevitably, found the in-box of her employers, Hobsons. The mood there became distinctly, well, moody.

'It is against company policy to send emails of an obscene nature,' a spokesman sniffily observed. 'This is a private and personal embarrassment for her, but I want to stress that the email represented Sharon's personal thoughts and not those of the rest of our staff.' Really? How does he know whether or not they like massage oil?

– ELECTRIC ATMOSPHERE –

Lightning kills an average of 100 people a year in the USA.

Afraid of lightning? Do yourself a favour. Don't read this next bit.

According to the National Oceanic and Atmospheric Administration, lightning kills an average of 100 people a year in the USA, making it the second biggest 'Weather Killer' in the country. That's more than hurricanes and tornadoes combined. Only floods do a better job for the Grim Reaper.

In fact, a quick browse through the NOAA's website produces some truly, er, striking information. Along with a lot of Inappropriate Capital Letters. For instance:

• Lightning Is The Number 1 Weather Killer in Florida – Killing More Than All Other Weather Sources Combined.

• If the gap between lightning and thunder is less than 30 seconds The Thunderstorm Is Close Enough To Be Dangerous.

• A House Or Other Fully Enclosed Substantially Constructed Building Offers Your Best Protection Against Lightning ['substantially constructed' means it has wiring and plumbing].

• A Car With A Metal Roof And Sides Is Your Second Best Protection Against Lightning… It Is The Metal Shell That Protects You, Not The Rubber Tires.

• Lightning Injures About 1,000 People In The US Each Year.

• Lightning Causes About $5 Billion Of Economic Impact In The US Each Year.

• Pennsylvania Leads The US In Lightning Damage.

- Long-term Lightning Symptoms Are Primarily Neurological And Are Difficult To Diagnose...Memory Deficit, Sleep Disturbance, Chronic Pain, Dizziness, And Chronic Pain (sic). Lightning Survivors Sometimes Have Trouble Processing Information, Are Easily Distracted, And have Personality Changes.

Finally, this gem which all average-lovers should cut out and keep in their scrapbooks:

- The Odds Of An Individual Being A Lightning Casualty In A Year In The US Is About 280,000-To-One – If You're An Average Person, In An Average Location, With Average Outside Activities, And Average Lightning Safety Behaviour. That's About 3000-To-One Over Your Lifetime, With About 300-To-One Odds Of Being Seriously Affected By A Family Member Or Friend Being A Lightning Survivor.'

Got that? The short version is: Don't Go Outside Ever. Especially if you're not sure whether your Outside Activities are Average and haven't recently swotted up on your Lightning Safety Behaviour.

Refreshing then to note the considerably far-from-average experience of UK pub manager Vincenzo Frascella, of Peterborough, Cambridgeshire, who played some literally electrifying golf at his local Orton Meadows club in 2003. He was struck by lightning twice *in the same round:* first while sheltering under an umbrella on the tricky 14th and again while negotiating the 17th. At this point even hardened golf addicts might have modified their Lightning Safety Behaviour and headed straight to the 19th for a quick stiffener. In fact, Vincenzo – handicap 25 – calmly completed his round.

'It's one of those things where you don't know whether you're lucky to be alive or unlucky to have been hit,' he said. 'I actually think I was a bit unlucky. I carried on and finished the round. I didn't think too much of it to be honest. I haven't been checked out or anything and I haven't felt any ill effects. I won't tell you my score. It was a bad day. But I don't think that was anything to do with the lightning – I just had a stinker.'

Vincenzo said he'd been told the chances of a double lightning strike on the same person were around three million to one. However researchers at the University of Arizona have just discovered that because lightning frequently hits the ground in two or more places, there are actually 1.45 strike points per flash. This means that your chances of getting struck are, on average, 45 per cent higher than previously thought.

Please, don't tell the Webmaster at NOAA.

– FRIENDS' FAREWELL –

US sitcom Friends *has been watched by almost a billion people in 60 countries.*

The extraordinarily successful series *Friends* encapsulated all the hopes and hang-ups of the have-it-all '80s generation – and yet all done with a light, comforting airhead touch. Of course, if you're not a *Friends* fan, it's all phooey. But most people have a favourite episode like they have a favourite pair of jeans.

So why did such a good thing have to end? According to Hollywood analysts the problem lies in producing original and *believable* story lines. They point to the demise of another classic US sitcom – *Happy Days,* starring Henry Winkler as The Fonz – in which a contrived and unconvincing plot has Winkler water-skiing over a man-eater straight from the set of *Jaws*. This rather desperate bit of scripting created a new Hollywood buzz-word – 'Jumping the Shark' – to describe the death throes of a dated show. Most experts reckon *Friends* jumped the shark long before the last of its 232 episodes.

But before completely dismissing Rachel, Joey, Monica, Chandler, Phoebe and Ross as one-dimensional comic stereotypes, take a peek at the show's financial numbers. Like 'em or loathe 'em, Planet Sitcom has nothing to touch 'em.

Since *Friends* made its debut on 22 September 1994, it has been watched by almost 1 billion people in more than 60 different countries. It is the most successful TV franchise in history. It has generated $3 billion in revenue for the NBC network and won 44 Emmys along the way. Props stolen from the set fetch anything up to £5,000 on the black market. Each 22-minute episode has a back-up team of 600 executives, technicians and writers.

By the end the six main stars were demanding – and got – contracts worth $1 million per show; the first sitcom cast ever to secure such a deal. Given that the final episode was watched by 51 million Americans, and US advertisers cheerfully forked out $2 million (£1.1 million) per 30-second slot, it's hardly surprising.

– MORE DOH! –

The success of *The Simpsons* has given the show's cast the kind of negotiating muscle rarely seen outside Hollywood's 'A-list' celebrity circle. Faced with the prospect of a strike by the likes of Dan Castellaneta (Homer) and Nancy Cartwright (Bart), producers Twentieth Century Fox TV reportedly doubled the salaries of the six main stars to an average $265,000 (£147,000) per episode for 2004. Over a typical 22-episode season that works out at $5.85 million (£3.25 million) a year – more than enough to keep Homer in beer and donuts.

– WORKING GIRLS –

About one person in every 300 in Germany is a hooker.

Prostitution is not only the oldest profession, it's also the hardest to analyse. This is because sex workers don't like cops or taxmen – at least, not unless they're clients – and so anonymity becomes the name of the game. Kind of.

That said, the European Union does have estimates for the average number of prostitutes working in member states. In some countries – notably France, The Netherlands, Luxembourg, Greece and Belgium – these figures are more like guess-timates, while in others – like Spain, Portugal and Ireland – there are no reliable figures at all! For the table at right we've taken the median between estimated highs and lows of the prostitute population where appropriate.

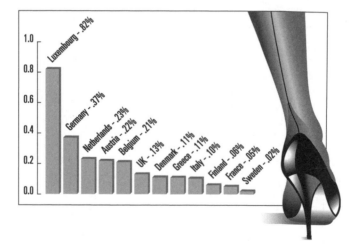

Percentage of population that work as prostitutes

Country	Number of citizens per prostitute
Luxembourg	121
Germany	266
Netherlands	421
Austria	457
Belgium	476
UK	750
Denmark	866
Greece	916
Italy	966
Finland	1500
France	2000
Sweden	3400

Leaving aside Luxembourg (where the ratio is skewed by large swings in the number of migrant sex workers), it's clear that Germany is the spiritual home of the hooker. There are 300,000 of them in a population of 80 million – a proportion clearly boosted by legalised brothels. Trouble is, when prostitution becomes legal it has to conform to rules. And no one makes a rule like the Germans.

So it is that German brothel-keepers have been ordered to conform to national laws requiring business to have one apprentice for every 15 workers. Assuming none of the existing 300,000 are going to be demoted, it means vacancies could exist for up to 20,000 apprentice prostitutes, male and female. This begs the following questions. What exams will they take to get qualified? Who'll do the marking? Are there to be specialist subjects? And will they need volunteers for the practical section?

On the other side of the pond, America's National Task Force on Prostitution suggests that over a million people have worked as prostitutes in the USA – around one per cent of American women. Though traditionally a female calling, the profile of the average sex worker is changing fast and it's no longer absolutely certain that the ones wearing mini-skirts are girls. In cities such as San Francisco, it's thought about a quarter of prostitutes are actually trans-gender. But, hey, if you're lonely, who's checking?

– CROSS PURPOSES –

Two-thirds of crossword puzzlers are women.

Here's a clue. Four down – *Angry noun challenge*. If you are one of the 40 million Americans and 8 million Britons who play at least one crossword puzzle a week, you'll have got that answer instantly. If not, well, TRY AGAIN, STUPID.

Publishers love crosswords because they help persuade advertisers that newspapers and magazines are upmarket and highbrow when, as we all know, they're in fact tacky and gossipy. Puzzles also particularly appeal to women (two-thirds of addicts are female) and the wealthy (the average income of US players is $72,000 or £49,000).

In Britain, where the cryptic puzzle was invented, crosswords played a curious role during World War II. They were used in 1942 to recruit intelligence officers for the task of breaking the Nazi Enigma code, an ultimately successful operation which turned the war in the Atlantic in the Allies' favour. Officers who could complete *The Daily Telegraph* crossword inside 12 minutes were seen as the 'right stuff'!

The *Telegraph* crossword also gave counter-intelligence agents at MI5 a nasty shock. Throughout the spring of 1944 puzzles included the following answers: Juno, Gold, Sword, Omaha, Overlord, Mulberry and Neptune. The first four of these were codenames for D-Day invasion beaches. Overlord was the name of the overall operation, Mulberry referred to floating harbours built for the landings and Operation Neptune was the naval assault phase.

Britain's spycatchers threw a wobbly, convinced that a Nazi agent had compromised security. They swooped on the crossword compiler, a mild-mannered headmaster called Leonard Dawe of Strand School, South London. In a later BBC interview, Dawe admitted: 'They turned me inside out.'

It seems the whole bizarre caper was a piece of good old-fashioned English farce. According to one of Dawe's pupils, Ronald French, the teacher would let boys insert words into his puzzle grids while he thought up clues to match them. By 1944 the entire school had been evacuated to Effingham, Surrey, and was next door to a huge camp of American and Canadian soldiers. These men used the code words openly – though they didn't know their significance. Ronald French, who spent his every spare moment in their company, simply passed the words on to his headmaster.

'Everyone knew the outline invasion plan and they knew the various code words,' he recalled later. 'Omaha and Utah were the beaches they were going to. They knew the names, but not the locations. We all knew the operation was called Overlord.'

'I was obviously not a German spy. Hundreds of kids must have known what I knew.'

– DOGGONE IT! –

How much is a dog worth? Anything up to 30 grand it seems. In the UK, research by Churchill Insurance suggests the average dog costs its owner £20,000 over a lifetime if you count feeding, grooming and vets' bills. The Great Dane weighs in at the most expensive – £30,000 over a typical ten-year lifespan – the result of a massive appetite and a propensity for hip and heart problems. Tightwad dog lovers should also give a long leash to boxers (higher risk of tumours), cavalier King Charles spaniels (tend to suffer obesity, heart and eye disease), basset hounds (obesity) and dalmations (urinary problems and deafness). Best bet is the English setter, a bargain at £18,910 over ten years, followed by Jack Russells, mongrels, English springer spaniels and poodle crosses. Or buy a goldfish.

– MOTH MAN –

On average one moth species becomes extinct in Britain every five years.

There are 120,000 species of moth known to man and, apparently, an estimated 120,000 still to be discovered. Yet fewer than ever before are found on Britain's shores. No one can be sure whether an apparently vanished species has in fact been overlooked, however we do know that their habitat is being eroded and that must play a part.

The vast majority of moths have a wingspan of less than 20 mm (1 inch)…which explains how one of them was able to fly into Antony Larose's ear.

Mr Larose, of Windsor, Berkshire, suffered excruciating pain as the trapped *lepidoptera* continually beat its wings against his eardrum. 'I've never been so scared – the noise was unimaginable,' he said. 'All I knew was that something with wings was trapped inside my ear and was doing its best to get out.'

His father-in-law tried to hose out the moth (surely *someone* in the family must have videoed this) but it took the gentle probing of doctors wielding tweezers to free the insect from its eerie experience.

– FAKING IT –

According to the European Central Bank, there's a one in 20,000 chance that any euro note in your wallet is a forgery. This doesn't sound too bad, but it's clearly enough to trouble the 55,000 retailers in Germany and Holland who now refuse to take the 100 euro (worth about £67 or $120 in proper money). According to the ECB, half a million fake notes worth £18.4 million were recovered in 2003, 50,000 of which were the 100 euro. Altogether there are 9 billion euro notes in circulation.

– HOME SWEET HOME –

The average British home earns more than the average British worker.

This, according to the figures from the Nationwide Building Society. With annual property inflation soaring to a heady 18.9 per cent in 2003/04, the typical home increased in value by £3,334 per month. Meanwhile, the country's average pre-tax monthly wage bumped along at £2,127.

However, before you rub your hands and bark a 'sell' order at your estate agent, do make sure your humble abode doesn't contain any sitting tenants. Specifically, dead ones.

In 1999 a couple who'd bought a 250-year-old cottage in Upper Mayfield, Derbyshire, sued the vendors for failing to reveal that the place was haunted. Andrew and Josie Smith launched a civil claim for £41,000 saying they had become aware of 'an evil presence'. Locals, they said, spoke of the cottage's disturbing history, including the suicide of a previous occupant.

The couple complained of an 'oppressive presence', sudden temperature swings, revolting smells, poltergeist activity, a feeling that they were being touched in their beds and a claim by one visitor that someone had 'walked through him'. At one stage Mrs Smith feared she was being 'throttled' by unseen hands while her husband told of a 'heavy atmosphere – so thick that you can lean into it'.

The judge threw out the case, citing a lack of hard evidence.

– SORRY FELLERS –

Bad news for timber smugglers (yes, they do exist) operating inside the protected Shimilipal forest sanctuary in Orissa, India. The trees form a vital habitat for tigers and pachyderms, yet on an average day some 6,000 tonnes are lost to a fellers' mafia. This haul is worth anything up to 120 million rupees (£1.8 million).

Now forest managers have had enough. Weary of ineffective security guards and the local police – all of whom complain that the gangs are too dangerous to tackle – they have trained three elephants to do the job instead. 'Unlike the guards, the elephants are not afraid,' one official told the Sify news agency. Nicking trunks is one thing. But trunks attached to tusks…?

– SNAIL MAIL –

Britain's Royal Mail loses letters at a rate of 40,000 per day.

At least you can usually work out where emails have ended up. Posting letters the old-fashioned way makes it much harder because Britain's Royal Mail tends to lose a lot of them. More precisely, it lost 14.4 million in 2002/03. And it's even worse when the article of mail you're waiting for is a tax rebate or one of those mail-order magazines sent in plain envelopes.

Horror stories about the postal system abound. One of our favourites, though: houses on one side of Moor Road North in Gosforth, Newcastle, England, had to wait three months for their mail, until the sorting office installed a new rack to cater for addresses with odd numbers. Then there's the postcard sent in 1908 to the Royal Hotel in Ventnor, Isle of Wight, England, asking for a room reservation. It arrived 96 years later.

– AND HOW DO YOU FEEL ABOUT THAT? –

More than 900 people a week seek help in brokering neighbour-hood disputes.

The Old Testament Commandment to 'Love Thy Neighbour' is proving a tricky one for many British citizens. According to Mediation UK, the agency which tries to settle disputes without recourse to expensive legal action, 47,000 Britons a year are seeking its services – more than 900 per week.

You can see how the agency's work might be challenging. In May 2004 Exeter Crown Court rejected 57-year-old Kenneth Gardener's appeal against his harassment conviction, ordered him to pay £2,445 in prosecution costs and banned him from going within 275 metres (300 yards) of neighbours Ashley and Maria Barlow's home in Pyworthy, Devon. Gardener had fallen out with the Barlows and took revenge by blocking their septic tank drainage, so denying them use of their toilet.

When Mr Barlow unblocked the drain and protected it with a manhole cover, Gardener got a pneumatic drill on the job. Then he poured soil and concrete into the drain and used a mechanical digger to pile earth onto the manhole cover making it inaccessible. In between times, he stuck on an Adolf Hitler-style moustache and paraded outside the Barlows' front door doing Nazi salutes. As they say in the mediation business...mediate *that*!

– MOVIE MAGIC –

Old movies are big money. More than two-thirds of the total $14.9 billion raked in from worldwide DVD film sales in 2003 came from back catalogues. This allowed the last major independent studio in Hollywood, MGM, to clock up $1 billion in revenues from its home entertainment division – an average of $2.7 million per day.

– CHILD'S PAY –

It costs an estimated £164,000 to bring up a child in Britain.

Everyone moans about the rising price of property. Yet it's still cheaper to buy the average UK house than it is to bring up the average UK kid.

In spring 2004, the cost of an average home was put at £146,000 compared with the £164,000 required to nurse junior through adolescence. Here's how the research from high street chain Woolworths adds up:

The harsh truth is that if you have three kids born over, say, a five-year period, then your maximum total payout in the most financially-crippling 5–11 period will be £35,000 per year. As that's roughly a third *more* than the average wage, it's hard to see how the numbers crunch up. Hard, that is, until you see the figures for UK credit card debt or read a book by Harvard University law professor Elizabeth Warren.

According to UK market analysts Datamonitor, the total outstanding debt on Britain's 65.5 million credit cards stood at £53.5 billion in 2003. That's £1,100 for every adult – up from £719 per adult in 1999. If current trends continue, there will be 90 million credit cards in circulation by 2008, an average of two per adult.

Warren's tome – depressingly titled *The Two Income Trap: Why Middle Class Mothers And Fathers Are Going Broke* – looks specifically at the American market, but could be applied to any Western economy. Warren found that US couples with children were 75 per cent more likely to be late paying bills, and twice as likely to file for bankruptcy, as childless couples.

* Gadgets in bedroom:

Games consoles	£600
Games	£1,470
TV/CD/DVD	£2,447
Computer	£1,000
Other gadgets	£1,000

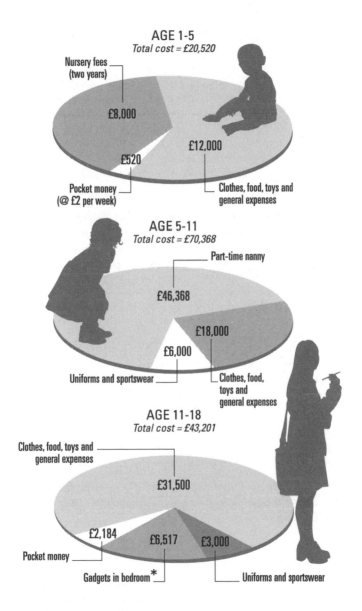

AGE 1-5
Total cost = £20,520

Nursery fees
(two years)

£8,000

£520

Pocket money
(@ £2 per week)

£12,000

Clothes, food, toys and
general expenses

AGE 5-11
Total cost = £70,368

Part-time nanny

£46,368

£18,000

£6,000

Uniforms and sportswear

Clothes, food,
toys and
general expenses

AGE 11-18
Total cost = £43,201

Clothes, food, toys and
general expenses

£31,500

£2,184

£6,517

£3,000

Pocket money

Gadgets in bedroom *

Uniforms and sportswear

– UGLY NAKED GUY –

About one in 50 Brits is a naturist.

According to various interpretations of a 2001 NOP opinion poll, there are some 1.2 million 'occasional' naturists in the UK, around one in 50 of the population. In the USA, 5 million is the conservative estimate. Let's face it, nudity is so cool it's goose-pimply. In fact, it's hard to get through the day without seeing someone, somewhere get naked.

Which may explain the big rush by pleasure boat passengers to get an eyeful of Splash Day, an event organised by the Austin Tavern Guild (a gay and lesbian group) at Hippie Hollow, the only public nude beach in Texas. In May 2004 the boat's passengers all crowded onto one side of their vessel to take in some real-life breasts and bottoms. Girl-on-girl or boy-on-boy action would obviously have been a bonus.

As you'd expect, the craft tipped over. Sixty people had to be rescued from Lake Travis. Is this why they call it Splash Day?

– DEADLY DIY –

Wallpapering sent an average of 400 Britons per day to accident and emergency rooms during Easter in 2003.

Great news for Do-It-Yourself dummies: DIY is dangerous and that's official.

Proof comes from the Royal Society for the Prevention of Accidents (ROSPA) in its analysis of mishaps for 2003. One of the truly shocking figures is that over the Easter weekend an average of 400 people PER DAY ended up in hospital accident and emergency departments with 'wallpapering' injuries.

These included one man who tried to remove wallpaper with a chopper (no sniggering please), one who used a carving knife and one who fell off a ladder onto his wife as she was cutting and pasting below. Overall, the most dangerous tools are apparently knives and scalpels (21,000 injuries), followed by saws (15,100), grinders (6,400) and hammers (5,800). In all, almost 250,000 DIY-ers ended up in hospital during 2003 and 70 of them died. [*]

Of these, perhaps the most tragic case involved 54-year-old electrician George Evans of Middlesbrough. His neighbour, Christopher Hoyland, stabbed him in the neck because he could no longer stand the noise of banging and drilling. Hoyland got ten years, reduced from 14, after the judge accepted he'd suffered brain damage in a previous fight.

– STICKY WICKET –

Cricketer Brian Lara scores an average 53.65 runs per test.

In 1988 West Lothian Cricket Club was casting around for an up-and-coming young West Indian player who could help coach their colts' side and give their league team an edge. They chose a slow bowler called Jerry Angus who went on to play 14 times for Guyana, taking

21 wickets and scoring 89 runs. He was a talented player, but his international career stalled with the emergence of all-rounders Carl Hooper and Roger Harper.

At West Lothian Angus got the nod over a 19-year-old batsman who'd played only two first-class matches. The club had asked a West Indies-based scout to watch this lad, but the report back was not encouraging. He lacked the technique and stamina to score a big innings and really didn't have the ability to play on Scottish wickets. His name? Ah yes, Brian Lara.

This would be the same Brian Lara then who holds the world record test score of 400 (against England in Antigua, 2004), who became the first player in Test Match history to twice hold the record for the highest individual innings, who is only the second player in history – behind the legendary Sir Donald Bradman – to score two triple Test hundreds in his career and who stands joint-second with Wally Hammond as scorer of most Test double centuries. God knows what he'd do if only he had technique, ability and stamina.

At the time of writing (summer 2004) Lara's test average stands at 53.65 – a truly outstanding return in the modern game. Few cricket fans would disagree that he is currently the greatest batsman in the world and this must surely rankle up in West Lothian. However, members there have gamely taken it on the chin.

'I suppose it was an error of judgement of some magnitude and makes me look a bit silly,' said committee member Gordon Hollins in one interview, 'but Jerry Angus stayed with us for two seasons and was very good.

'However Lara really is something else, a phenomenal batter, almost freakish in the range of boundary shots he can play. The better he gets the more he will haunt me. I can't remember the name of the scout in Trinidad now. But I know we gave him the sack.'

– KEEPING IT IN THE FAMILY –

'Bob's your uncle' is one of those peculiarly British phrases used to affirm that everything is just fine. You've probably heard the phrase scores of time without even having an uncle called Bob. However, Arthur Balfour did have an uncle named Bob when he got the plum job as Secretary of State for Ireland back in 1887. It was Robert Cecil, Lord Salisbury, the incumbent prime minister. Thus having an uncle called Bob became a symptom of good fortune.

– SUMMER BABES –

If you're a single man dreading the effect babies will have on your wallet (ie, *all* single men) then listen up. A study of 3,000 Austrian women by Dr Susanne Huber of the University of Veterinary Medicine in Vienna has revealed that women born in June, July and August are, on average, less fertile than non-summer borns. There are several theories – colder weather, poorer winter nutrition, exposure to winter diseases – all of which might affect early foetal development.

Big question is, though: why do Austrian women see vets instead of doctors?

– STRESS BILL –

City traders in London carry out an average of 61,500 transactions a day.

This 2004 figure was up 60 per cent from the same period the year before – and the deals go on, despite the high stress levels that come with the job.

Stress often wrecks stockbrokers' employees' lives, but it can also prove costly for their employers. A City of London trader working for Commerzbank, 36-year-old Helen McNallen, left her desk early on 3 January 2000 because of a stress-related illness. All had seemed quiet on the Italian futures market, but after Miss McNallen left there was a sudden collapse in prices. The immediate loss was £3.98 million, offset only slightly by later trading.

Miss McNallen was suspended when she arrived for work the following day. She then sued the bank for £1 million in damages, claiming she became suicidal through work-related stress. An undisclosed out-of-court settlement was agreed in April 2004.

– LASHING OUT –

It's a common misconception that a room that's too small to swing a cat has dimensions that fall far short of the average whiskers-to-tail length of a feline. Actually, the cat in question is a cat 'o' nine tails once used to mete out floggings. A few centuries ago this was the punishment of choice in the British navy and it would be carried out on deck in front of the rest of the crew. That's because, below deck, there wasn't sufficient room to swing a cat. The term 'over a barrel' is strongly linked to land-locked whippings that often occurred as the victim was being towed on a cart around town. His arms would be lashed to the far side of a wooden barrel so, with his feet planted on the cart floor, the target area – his back – was made more prominent.

– BOOKED IN –

According to America's National Coalition for the Homeless, 1.35 million US children – average age nine – are without a home on any given night.

Of the young people identified as homeless by State Education Departments, 35 per cent live in shelters, 34 per cent shack up with family or friends and 23 per cent live in motels or other locations. 'Other locations', it turns out, include university libraries.

In one of those strange-but-true stories which we gobble up here in the *Lore Of Averages* editorial office, a 20-year-old homeless man called Steve Stanzak spent eight months sleeping in the New York University library. The creative-writing student camped out on four chairs, washed in the toilets, kept all his possessions in a locker and recounted his experiences on a website under the heading: 'The tale of a penniless boy's quest to gain a college education'.

While nobody noticed him snoring in the Bobst Library, plenty of people noticed him on the Internet. This clearly says something about today's society, but at least NYU officials acted fast when his site was pointed out to them. Stanzak was offered free digs in a hall of residence.

Later he revealed the downside of his library stint. 'I can't concentrate in Bobst because I've become so comfortable,' he said. 'If I have a lot of studying to do, I'll go to McDonald's.'

– ONE-ARMED BANDIT –

Drunken drivers kill or injure 54 people a day in Britain.

To help combat this dire statistic, police carried out 570,000 'screening' breath tests on motorists in 2002, 9 per cent fewer than the previous year. Yet the number of positive tests actually *rose* by 4 per cent to 103,000. This means the cops now catch an average of 282 over-the-limit drivers every day. How many thousands slip through the net?

This one didn't: The man who called Liverpool police and reported the theft of his steering wheel, pedals and dashboard had both good news and bad news awaiting him. The good news was that he had got into the back seat instead of the front and that the steering wheel was safe and sound, just where he'd left it. The bad news was the police arrived to arrest him on a suspicion of drink-driving after he rang them back to share his bit of good news.

Of course, drink-driving is bad enough, but some motorists don't see why there should be any motoring laws. Take Stuart MacNamara of Swansea, South Wales. In 2001 he was caught driving with double the legal level of alcohol in his blood while jumping a red light and making a call on his mobile phone. There was an additional problem in that he only had one arm...and it was the one holding the phone. His car was not adapted to cater for his disability, which presumably means he was steering with his knees. Either that or...no, let's move on.

MacNamara got an 18-month ban, together with fines and costs totalling £450. South Wales Police head of traffic Superintendent Dick Lewis said afterwards: 'Each offence is bad enough in its own right, but in combination they are more severe. The recklessness of this driver leaves me speechless.'

Across the Atlantic the war on drink-driving is going rather better. The number of alcohol-related traffic fatalities more than halved from an average 1.64 deaths per 161 million km (100 million miles) driven in 1982 to just 0.61 deaths in 2002. In 2001 traffic cops arrested 3,835 drivers per day for alcohol or drugs violations – a rate of one for every 137 licensed drivers in the USA.

Drink-driving can be a deliberate and dangerous act, whereas minor motoring offences rarely put lives in jeopardy. It's important that courts are *seen* to recognise the difference, which is why Columbia City Judge Tom DuBois's approach to justice is so refreshing.

Every Christmas Judge DuBois strikes a deal with minor offenders in Tennessee. He lets them off without a fine provided they stand up in court and sing a Christmas carol. *Jingle Bells*, *Rudolph The Red-Nosed Reindeer* and *We Wish You A Merry Christmas* are among the favourites.

'Some people need a little help with their tunes,' observes Judge DuBois, 'so we sometimes have duets and even quartets. Our court officer, Kenny Lovett, sometimes helps people out. He sings in his church choir.'

– BIBLICAL PROPORTIONS –

The average number of new bibles sold or given away in the USA works out at 168,000 per day.

At this rate the entire population could get a new copy once every four years, which would produce a typical lifetime collection of around 17.

Unsurprisingly, Bible statistics are heaven on Earth to keen students. According to various Internet sources – and if they've fibbed they could be in big trouble one day – the 66 books of the Old and New Testaments contain on average 471 verses, 11,865 words, 121 predictions, 50 fulfilled prophecies, 48 unfilled prophecies, 50 questions, 19 promises and 98 commands. The word 'God' appears on average 50 times per book and 'Lord' 117 times.

Finding printing errors in Bible text is a painstaking business and so it's a big *hallelujah* to the sharp-eyed proofreaders at Peachtree Editorial and Proofreading in Georgia. Among the typographical howlers they spotted in a new edition of the Good Book were 'sour ancestors', instead of 'our ancestors', and an end to 'fractions' rather than 'factions'. 'Bible readers are less forgiving of errors because they expect perfection in the Bible text,' said Peachtree owner June Gunden.

– BORIS BELCHER –

Beer sales in Russia have risen by a fifth in less than five years.

For centuries Russia has been synonymous with vodka. Now new figures from the country's drinks industry suggest that exposure to Western culture has given beer a cool new image. Whereas spirits – and for 'spirits' read 'vodka' – accounted for three-quarters of Russian alcohol sales in 2000, they notched up a comparatively paltry 67.3 per cent in 2003. Beer sales on the other hand are booming at an annual rate of 20 per cent to stand at 23.8 per cent of the total market. That's up from 17.4 per cent in 2000.

This is all good news for Russia's biggest brewer Baltika, valued at £1.1 billion in 2004. The company's market share has increased by an average 1.5 per cent every year since 1994, ensuring that its president and privatisation mastermind Taimuraz Bolloyev is well up Russia's elite league of the nouveau riche.

– FLIPPIN' HECK –

Emperor penguin chicks have a 50 per cent survival rate.

It's a hard life being a penguin. Take the emperor species, for example. The male bird feeds on fish, squid and krill, and sometimes has to dive as deep as 518 metres (1,700 feet) to find them. It manages this on one lungful of air (which it can hold for up to 18 minutes), all the time dodging the killer whales and leopard seals who like a toothsome bit of emperor penguin when they can get it.

Mating – which you'd think might lighten things up – is the opposite of a warm, sharing experience. In winter, as the skies darken and the temperature plummets, the male emperor trudges across the ice to find a nesting place. The female emperor rolls over her egg and waddles off with some girlie pals on a fishing jolly. He then stands on the ice, egg balanced on his feet, for nine weeks. During this time the mercury can drop to -60°C (-76°F), the wind-speed can touch 160 kph (100 mph) and there's not the remotest chance of a bite to eat.

When the chick finally hatches, there's only half a chance of it surviving to adulthood. Most starve to death, and soaring average temperatures in the Antarctic – up from -17°C (1.4°F) 50 years ago to -15°C (5°F) today – have only made matters worse. The melting ice means there's fewer places to forage for food.

With all these factors conspiring against the penguin, you might hope the scientists would be on their side. Not so. During nine summer seasons between 1987 and 1996, around 36,000 penguins of ten different species were 'banded' by researchers working on various conservation projects. They attached metal bands to the birds' flippers to monitor activity and find ways of improving survival rates.

It seems there's just one slight problem. According to a review by French scientists published in the Royal Society journal *Biology Letters* in 2004, king penguin chicks are twice as likely to die young if they are banded. And placing a single flipper band on an Adelie penguin reduces its swimming efficiency by more than one-fifth. Why don't they just tie weights to the poor little things and be done with it?

– REVENGE OF THE FISH –

During the first two weeks that marine-themed cartoon Finding Nemo *was released on DVD, it netted an average sale of 1,080,000 copies a day.*

Not only was *Finding Nemo* a box office sensation in 2003 – becoming one of the top 20 biggest films ever – it was soon a must for home entertainment, too. Copies of the DVD flew off the shelves, with 15 million selling in the first two weeks after its release, as well as an additional 5 million copies of the video.

This is not surprising really, for the film's characters are cute, the story is rousing, the comedy is refreshingly original and the animation is superb. What is surprising is the way that digital art has mirrored life.

Finding Nemo is about a father's search for his missing son. Their reunion is marred when nets close around a mighty catch of fish and it's 'destination dinner plate' for at least one of the film's heroes. But bold little Nemo knows that if all the captured fish swim down in a singular effort they will find freedom once more and this is exactly what happens. When the fish head south, the bar supporting the massive fishing net breaks and the haul escapes. Curiously this is almost precisely what happened in real life to one Norwegian vessel.

Fishermen on the 10-metre (62-foot) *Steinholm* were delighted to net a massive haul of herring in their nets off Norway's northern coast. The smiles were quickly wiped from their faces as the fish dived as one for the ocean floor and capsized the vessel. Six crewmen tried in vain to sever the nets, but swiftly had to abandon ship. From lifeboats they watched as the *Steinholm* sank in ten minutes. They were rescued soon afterward by another trawler. Captain Geir Nikolaisen observed: 'I have been fishing since I was 14 and I have never heard of anything like it.'

– VINTAGE PHOBIA –

On average people fear spiders more than they fear death.

Given that there are some 40,000 different kinds of spiders in the world and there's almost certainly one not far from where you are right now, it is ridiculous but true that usually people's arachnophobia is more acute than their concerns about shuffling off this mortal coil. Of the multitude of types of spiders that exist, only about 30 are poisonous to humans, the most venomous being the Brazilian huntsman. However, an anti-venom has been developed and few die after becoming spider-fodder. In fact, statistics tell us that you are more likely to be killed by a champagne cork than by a poisonous spider. Mind you, champagne corks don't come up the plughole in the bath...

– MR SANDBOY –

The phrase 'happy as a sandboy' is often uttered without anyone asking the obvious question, who or what is a sandboy? He was apparently an early health-and-safety operative. The saying stems from the days when sand was the height of good hygiene in local inns, being spread across the floor to absorb spills, spit and sweat. At beachside pubs young lads were sent by landlords to collect sand from the shore, being paid in ale to do so. Thus the sandboys were happily intoxicated.

– LOTTO PROBLEMS –

The odds of predicting six consecutive balls chosen out of 50 in a lottery game amounts to 15,890,700 to one.

There's plenty of reasons not to take part in a lottery. A battery of figures has been produced to show the chances of winning are laughably remote, not least that you have as much chance of selecting a lucky coin from a row of 10 pence pieces lying side by side over a distance of 352 km (220 miles) as you do of picking the lucky line. Nevertheless, there are plenty of us willing to risk some fairly paltry stake money in an against-all-odds bid to drastically alter our personal circumstances. Miraculous events mostly don't happen. Occasionally they do, but not always in the way you'd imagined.

Maureen Wilcox might have been forgiven for thinking that somebody up there didn't like her when the numbers she selected for the Massachusetts lottery came up in the Rhode Island draw. But imagine her chagrin when she discovered the numbers she picked for the Rhode Island lottery came up – guess where? That's right, they were the winning line in neighbouring Massachusetts. She chose no fewer than two winning lines in January 1998, yet her cash rewards amounted to a big, fat zero.

Buddy Post probably wishes he had won nothing at all, instead of scooping $16.2 million in the Pennsylvania State Lottery in 1988. For with his big windfall came a string of personal disasters. His former landlady Ann Carpic made a claim on the jackpot, saying she shared the ticket with him. While legal proceedings plodded on, the payment of the winnings was suspended and mounting legal bills led the Oil City man swiftly into debt. That might have been manageable if only his sixth wife had not left him. Then Post discovered his own brother had plotted to kill him to get his hands on the cash. Post was himself convicted of assault as he fired a shotgun in the near vicinity of his step-daughter's boyfriend. By this time he was probably dreaming of his former life as a humble cook in the way that most of us fantasise about winning the lottery. As Post succinctly put it: 'Money draws flies.'

Just to prove that state lotteries are not immune from downright spooky happenings, a Canadian newspaper once printed the winning line of the Oregon lottery before it was drawn. The relevant numbers were inserted in error after a technical glitch put newspaper producers in a spin. In fact, it was the numbers necessary for Virginia's jackpot. When Oregon's numbers came up some hours after the newspaper was published, the same sequence occurred.

However, it's not entirely a tale of woe. In Australia a grandfather proved that luck moved in mysterious ways when he won the lottery three times over on the same draw. He bought one ticket before going abroad to celebrate his 60th birthday. In confusion about the date of the draw he asked a friend in his home city of Sydney to purchase another with the same numbers. And on his return from overseas he bought the third, once again with the same sequence. He was one of 20 with winning numbers – but the only one with three times as many tickets as everyone else.

In the same continent truck driver Bill Morgan, 37, won a £10,800 (A$27,000) car through a scratch card. Asked by a local television station to re-enact the triumph in front of the cameras he picked up another scratch card and won £100,000 (A$250,000). The lottery company worked out that Mr Morgan had a one in 6.1 billion chance of winning the pair of prizes. He believed his luck was down to an earlier coronary in which his heart stopped for 14 minutes, permitting his late mother to once again exert an influence on his life.

In France a father and daughter, living 320 km (200 miles) apart, independently picked the winning line of the lottery to split £6 million. If that was not coincidence enough, the father was the nephew of France's first-ever lottery winner, who scooped the jackpot back in 1933.

If it helps, at the time of going to press the most picked winning numbers in the British national lottery game in descending order were 38, 44, 43, 25, 47 and 23. The least picked in ascending order were 13, 20, 41, 21, 16 and 37. I don't think that helps.

– AND FINALLY... –

The number of cults existing in the USA today stands at between 1,000–5,000.

In Great Britain there are about 500 cults functioning, while in Japan the figure stands at 180,000. The figures don't mean much, really, for cults can spring up and vanish with alarming speed. Few of the leaders are keen to broadcast their activities either.

Some cults are benign and merely offer a degree of comfort to members. Others are mighty with claims that are sufficient to scare the living daylights out of most right-thinking people.

On the say-so of some self-appointed heavenly messengers, many human beings have been convinced that the end of the world is nigh. To date, they have all been disappointed.

DAYS OF JUDGMENT GONE BY...

Cult	Leader
31 December 2000	
The Movement for the	'Bishop' Joseph Kibwetere
Restoration of the Ten	'Sister' Credonia Mwerinde
Commandments of God	Father Dominic Kataribabo
August 2000	
World Message Last	Wilson Bushara
Warning Church	
December 1999	
Concerned Christians	Monte Kim Miller
31 March 1998	
God's Salvation Church	Hon-Ming Chen
or God Saves the Earth	
Flying Saucer Foundation	
or Chen Tao (True Way)	
26 March 1997	
Heaven's Gate	Marshall H Applewhite
20 March 1995	
Aum Supreme Truth	Shoko Asahara
19 April 1993	
Branch Davidians	David Koresh
18 November 1978	
The People's Temple	Jim Jones
Various	
Order of the Solar	Luc Jouret
Temple	Joseph di Mambro

– SISTER ACT –

To maintain the current population, women must produce an average of 2.1 children apiece.

Making babies often defies logic and planning. What were the chances, then, when Tracy Harrison, 27, and her sister Vicky, 19, produced offspring at the exact same moment in the same hospital? Tracy had a son, James, weighing 3.26 kg (7 lb 3 oz) in Darlington Memorial Hospital, England, while Vicky gave birth to 3 kg (6 lb 12 oz) daughter Chloe, both at the same special moment in 1998.

The births were good news, and not just for mums Tracy and Vicky. The birthrate in the Western world is plummeting, with fewer babies being born than ever before. Here's the thing. If women produce more than 2.1 children, the population will rise. But when the figure is less, population falls, the old will outnumber the young and international economics will go haywire. According to Future Foundation, the fertility rate in the USA is 1.93 per female. And frankly that looks great against that of the UK (1.6), Japan (1.3) Germany (1.29) and Italy (1.2), while things are so bad in Australia that some newspaper headlines have announced 'Aussies face extinction'.

They are among 62 countries worldwide in this unenviable position of negative equity on babies. England enjoyed a brief respite in February 2003 when there was a statistical surge in the number of babies born. The significance of this was, of course, soccer's World Cup taking place in Japan nine months previously. It wasn't the game between England and Brazil that fired the passions of the nation's men. The goal lofted past David Seaman by Brazilian hero Ronaldinho was a definite turn-off.

No, it was the one–nil victory over Argentina on 2 June 2002 that got the fellas going. It was the goal scorer David

Beckham that did it for the women and the outcome was an unknown number of ecstatic liaisons. The consequent statistical blip in the birthrate has been tagged 'the Beckham boom'. Never has one man done so much for so many on the field of sporting endeavour.

If our only hope for survival as a species is that England wins the World Cup, then the future indeed looks bleak. We have to keep it real here, folks. But before you all rush off to make babies in celebration of an Accrington Stanley home win, the news may not be all bad. One theory is that a smaller population will make fewer demands on the natural world. (Never forget that a human eats about 60,000 pounds of food in its lifetime, the equivalent weight of six elephants.) So by depopulating we are helping to save the planet. Let's wait and see...

– CARD TRICKS –

Genteel village whist drives are generally short on awesome shocks. But not when cardsharps met at Bucklesham, near Ipswich in Suffolk, one winter's evening in 1998. Hilda Golding, 87, could barely disguise her astonishment when she discovered her hand contained all 13 of the pack's clubs. Playing partners Hazel Ruffles, 64, and her daughter Alison Chilvers, 40, had all the diamonds and hearts respectively. The spades all went into the dummy hand. According to one pseudo statistician before World War II, the odds against this happening are 2,235,197,406,895,366,368,301,599,999 to one. To satisfy the cynics among you, the pack in question had been shuffled and cut.

– FEEL THE FORCE –

A female orgasm lasts for between five and eight seconds.

As with every other area of sex, the orgasm has been dissected, charted, measured and analysed. Consider yourself an average Joe or Josephine? Then compare yourself to the figures worked out by sex investigator Alfred Kinsey.

He found that three-quarters of all men reached orgasm within two minutes of penetration and that it lasted no more than five seconds.

Women could bring themselves to orgasm in just under four minutes, although that time span increased to anything up to 20 minutes during intercourse.

The power of the orgasm has never been more succinctly illustrated than by Meg Ryan in the film *When Harry Met Sally*. In one of cinema's most memorable scenes, she mimics a climax during dinner at a restaurant, to the embarrassment of her pal, played by Billy Crystal, and the bemusement of other diners.

The potent scene re-enacted for a stage play in London's West End appears to have taken its toll on the very fabric of the theatre. In May 2004 a performance at the Theatre Royal in the Haymarket was disrupted when a chandelier sheered away from the ceiling bringing a shower of plasterwork with it. The show's star Luke Perry helped to evacuate the audience. Although 13 people went to hospital, further casualties were prevented by a safety rope, which kept the chandelier aloft.

– BLOOMING AMAZING –

On average we spend 90 per cent of our time indoors.

Which is curious when you consider how much money we spend making our gardens gorgeous, to spend no more than 10 per cent of our day there. The most money goes on lawn care, with American homeowners spending an average of $220 on associated products. The next most costly item on the shopping list, according to one set of US statistics, is landscaping, which adds up to an annual budget of $174, then care for existing trees, costing $97 per annum.

The bill for flowers stands at $88 per household, while $60 is forked out each year on pest control. These are figures that must stick in the throat of one English gardener whose glorious garden display in the picturesque county of Devon withered and died virtually before her eyes.

At first Sarah Potter suspected drought, then disease. But upon inspection she realised that neither could have been to blame for the sudden death syndrome now at large in her garden. She suspected human intervention – and used a camcorder to catch neighbours Ian and Marie Davey tipping poison onto the plot.

On one occasion she videoed Marie Davey pouring liquid from a teacup over the plants while Davey's husband kept watch on the pavement. The following morning it was Ian Davey's turn to act as poisoner while his wife stood guard.

In August 1994 the Daveys admitted causing criminal damage in Mrs Potter's garden in Silverton, Exeter. They told police they bought sodium chlorate for the task, believing Mrs Potter had damaged their plants. They were given a 12-month conditional discharge and ordered to pay £60 compensation.

– THE WRITE WAY WITH ENGLISH –

The average novel sells 2,000 copies.

The publishing world has been turned on its head by a hike in sales in children's books, particularly those written by one specific author. JK Rowling tapped a vein when she created the wizard Harry Potter. Consequently, when the latest tome in the series was released on 21 June 2003, no fewer than 1,679,753 people rushed off to buy it. One in every 35 British people possessed a copy of *Harry Potter And The Order Of The Phoenix* by close of trading that day. It's something of a similar story across the pond. In America overall book sales in consumer publishing – that includes children's books – rose by 6.3 per cent in 2003.

Rowling has been a hit over there, too, along with fellow Brit, Lynne Truss. Hers was one of the surprise bestsellers of the publishing world in 2003 and one of the most imaginatively titled. *Eats, Shoots And Leaves* is a warm and witty defence of English punctuation. Subtitled 'The Zero Tolerance Approach to Punctuation', it not only topped the charts in the UK, but also surfaced across the Atlantic atop *The New York Times'* non-fiction list. In the three months after it was launched in America the publisher went back to press 16 times, pushing the total number of copies to 795,000. Its intriguing title came from an old joke about a panda who walked into a café, had a sandwich and fired a gun before exiting the establishment. Asked why he acted so strangely he advised the questioner look up the entry next to his name in a wildlife manual – and it read: 'Panda. Large black-and-white bear-like mammal, native to China. Eats, shoots and leaves.'

Ms Truss is not alone in waging war on English language bandits. There also exists the Apostrophe Protection Society, which hit the headlines with its vocal backing for Nottingham City councillors and staff who agreed to donate £2 to charity every time they abused the apostrophe.

Alternatively, there are some signs that need more than a grammatical overhaul. The words need to be rubbed out and the writer should start all over again.

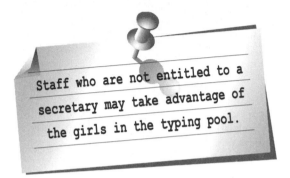

Staff who are not entitled to a secretary may take advantage of the girls in the typing pool.

At a beauty salon: 'Ears pierced while you wait.'

At a garage: 'Hot wash with attendant.'

On an office noticeboard: 'Staff who are not entitled to a secretary may take advantage of the girls in the typing pool.'

Outside a farm: 'Bag your own manure.'

On the side of a mincemeat jar: 'The contents are sufficient for a pie for six persons or 12 small tarts.'

On a pill bottle: 'Take one capsule with each loose stool – max 8 daily.'

In a newspaper report: 'Fun entertainment that will have Lincoln children riveted to the stage.'

On a Swedish chainsaw: 'Do not attempt to stop chain with your hands or genitals.'

Perhaps the worst sign ever written was penned not in English but in the tongue of the Filipinos. It was written on behalf of dignitaries in San Jose, California, to welcome a group of businessmen from the Philippines and it should have read 'Tuloy po kayo' meaning 'Welcome Filipinos'. What it actually said was 'Tuley po kayo' meaning 'Circumcise Filipinos' – not the same thing at all.

– YOU SAY POTATO... –

Sometimes we use language to flummox rather than clarify. This mainly happens with job titles, all too frequently given in lieu of a pay rise. Some of our favourite examples:

Technical Sanitation Assistant – lavatory cleaner
Stock Replenishment Executive – shelf stacker
In Home Infant Protection Executive – babysitter
Carriage Movement Facilitator – station porter

– POURQUOI? –

There's two distinct schools of thought about the origin of the somewhat ludicrous command to 'mind your p's and q's'. The first holds that it was sound advice to pub customers who were served in pints and quarts, at a time when the amount they owed was kept on a tab. The more pints they consumed the more hazy they became over the sum owed and unscrupulous innkeepers would begin charging for quarts instead of pints. However, it also sits nicely with an explanation that has 'p' meaning 'please' and 'q' being the central syllable of 'thank you'. It then becomes a swift parental reminder to children to remember their 'please's and 'thank you's.

– ANIMAL LOVERS –

On average 273 hedgehogs are killed daily on British roads.

The British are known for being soft on small, cute creatures. Yet the nation's drivers run over an average of 273 hedgehogs every day. It's a shame, that, for hedgehogs are curiously fascinating animals.

You might never see one doing it, but hedgehogs can apparently swim and climb trees. If they fall from a branch they don't exactly bounce like a ball, but their spines do give them a soft landing.

You might never hear it, but hedgehogs hiss like snakes when they are confronted by predators, although more usual noises in the hedgehog repertoire are snorting, grunting, coughing and sneezing.

These snouty animals have always inspired respect – perhaps even envy – for their ability to hibernate in the winter. It means modifying their heart rate from 190 beats per minute to just 20 to survive the lengthy period of cold inactivity.

Apart from rolling them flat, humans have pursued hedgehogs to gather their urine, which was once thought a cure for baldness. Some chose to eat hedgehog meat in the belief that it cured poisoning and averted evil. A final hedgehog fact – and it's an easy one to remember. A group of hedgehogs is rightly termed 'a prickle'.

– SAND FOLLIES –

The most successful sandcastles have one part water to eight parts sand.

Those who want to be king of the sandcastle will be intrigued to hear of research carried out by a professor from Bournemouth University on behalf of Teletext Holidays on the best way to build a sandcastle. During his research, Professor Matthew Bennett used the special formula OWO.125 x s – that's one part water to eight parts sand to you and me.

He explained: 'The strength of a sandcastle depends on how the grains interact, so the correct mix of sediment and water is crucial to any castle that is being built. Too much water and the sand will liquefy. Too little water and the sand won't bind.'

This will doubtless save much head-scratching among the nation's under-fives during their scientific dabbling on the beach with buckets and spades.

The top five British beaches for sandcastle building were:

1. Torquay, Devon
2. Bridlington, East Yorkshire
3. Great Yarmouth, Norfolk
4. Bournemouth, Dorset
5. Tenby, Pembrokeshire

Building sandcastles on the beach is no longer child's play, as scores of mighty and ornate structures are fashioned every year on beaches across the world. Today's castles have turrets, crenellations and drawbridges, and are peopled by armies on horseback. Forming such intricate structures takes man-sized shovels and even mechanical diggers, when builders were once content with battlements that came in a pre-formed bucket and a moat they could dig with a plastic spade.

To talk in terms of definitive world records is meaningless, as the heights and sheer weight of sand in competitive sculpturing are being increased with each passing year. (That's without going into details of mechanised or hand built, inside or outdoors and so forth.) The dimensions of the following castles are worthy of consideration, though:

- In 1999 no fewer than 90 US and Dutch sculptors created a sand scene entitled 'A meeting with the Greek gods' that was 70 metres (230 feet) wide, 100 metres (328 feet) long and 17.28 metres (56' 8") tall.

- A hand-built sandcastle constructed inside 100 man-hours at Stone Mountain Park, Georgia, was 8.58 metres (28' 7") tall and weighed 225 tonnes.

- In New York State fairgrounds a sandcastle was built under cover, during a 17-day spell, that measured 10.2 metres (33' 6") and weighed 412 tonnes.

It was these sand monuments that inspired German tourist Mario Dreher and two friends to build a twin-towered castle standing 2.33 metres (7.6 feet) tall surrounded by a 1.8-metre (6-foot) deep moat on a Dutch beach in July 1994. He even decorated the entrance with seashells.

But as he jumped in the moat to look up at his fantastic handiwork it collapsed on top of him, burying him alive.

Watching tourists leapt into action when they realised the 24-year-old could not burrow himself out. Forty of them dug furiously with their hands and discovered him three minutes later already unconscious. He was rushed to hospital in Nordwijk, Holland, where he was revived in an oxygen tent.

Later Mario said: 'Our building plans were a bit too ambitious. Now we'll just spend the rest of the holiday sitting quietly on the beach.'

Campaigners on the hidden dangers of sand holes are quick to point out that seven people were trapped by sand collapse on New England beaches in the six years between 1996 and 2002. Along the same stretch of coastline there have been seven shark attacks in 300 years.

– HOT STUFF –

Today the expression 'getting fired' has profound, rather than tragic, implications. If you have recently been made jobless and are down in the dumps, spare a thought for those who got 'fired' years ago when the phrase first came into being. It was in an era when villagers who grew tired of pesky neighbours got rid of them by burning their house down; an extreme response, but one that clearly occurred often enough for the phrase to be absorbed into common usage.

– CONGRATULATIONS, EJACULATIONS –

An estimated 1.2 trillion sperm are produced in every man during his lifetime.

The fact that fewer babies are coming into the world is a credit to birth control measures that are more varied and effective than ever before. It also reflects an apparent increase in the biological problems that might affect would-be parents.`

For those wishing to conceive, but finding themselves unable to do so, it is no comfort to know that the average male body produces something in the region of 72 million sperm a day – and it only takes one squiggly tadpole to make a baby. With every ejaculation a man says goodbye to between 200 and 600 million sperm swimming at speeds of up to 4 mm (0.25 inches) a minute.

Of course, it helps to send them off in the right direction. A sperm will live for no more than two days inside a woman, but that compares well to the two-minute lifespan they enjoy after hitting the bed sheets.

Although the farthest-known ejaculation recorded semen travelling an astonishing 3.5 metres (11 feet, 5 inches), it does help to be in the vicinity of the intended mother of your child.

– BITE ME –

Nowadays, 'biting the bullet' is a phrase that denotes the acceptance of a punishment. It comes from the days when those who were being whipped would bite on a real bullet to prevent them shrieking or biting their tongues while the flogging was administered. Bullets were also sometimes given to patients to bite on while early surgical practices – too grim to discuss here – were carried out without the benefit of anaesthetic. Yet there are some that hold that the saying was born out of disgraceful practices in Britain's empire days. Back then, bullets had to be parted so the base could be filled with gunpowder, and the easiest way to do this under fire was through biting the cartridge apart. To speed everything up, all working parts were greased with pig or cow fat. This presented no problem to Anglican troops, but was a major obstacle for Hindu and Muslim soldiers who were prohibited by faith to consume products from the animals in question. Nevertheless, commanding officers held it was better to fight for the British Empire than to observe their religion – and that's mostly why the Indian Mutiny broke out in 1857, which was characterised by bloody massacres on both sides.

– PENIS POWER –

The average erect penis length is 156.4 mm or 6.16 inches.

Sperm is delivered by that cunningly designed tool, the penis. But when it comes to the law of averages, penises are all over the place. Most men pride themselves on the length of their penis, others are acutely embarrassed by it. In reality the range of lengths and girths is broad and the average willy is hard to find.

The chart at right shows some statistics gathered by The Alfred C Kinsey Institute for Sex Research on erect penis lengths among white college students. The research, done decades ago, with men marking the size of their erect penises on a stamped, address postcard and sending it in, has been the benchmark in penis statistics for two generations.

The mathematicians among you won't need reminding then that the average erect penis length is 6.16 inches (156.4 mm), while the average girth measures up to 4.84 inches (122.9 mm). Except that another study, this time conducted at the University of California in San Francisco, found that the average size of erect penises in its 'guinea pig' group was just 5.1 inches (129.5 mm) while the girth was a more impressive 4.9 inches (124.4 mm). Not so, says a urologist from Brazil who discovered from a group of 150 men that the average size, when erect, of their penises was 5.7 inches (144.7 mm), the girth being almost exactly 1 inch (25 mm) less at 4.7 inches (119.3 mm). Enter Lifestyles Condom Company and its research, which has the average penis at 5.877 inches (149.27 mm). That was deduced from a survey of 300 men in Cancun, Mexico, with a population boosted by US visitors during the spring break. The average girth came in at 4.972 inches (126.28 mm). Spokesman Simon Joseph said: 'Our results show that about three-quarters of men fall under the average quoted by Kinsey. A half-inch or less might not have anything to do with how you perform sexually, but it might make a difference in how you feel about yourself.'

Percentage	Population icons	Size
0.2%		3.75"
0.3%		4"
0.2%		4.25"
1.7%		4.5"
0.8%		4.75"
4.2%		5"
4.4%		5.25"
10.7%		5.5"
8%		5.75"
23.9%		6"
8.8%		6.25"
14.3%		6.5"
5.7%		6.75"
9.5%		7"
1.8%		7.25"
2.9%		7.5"
1%		7.75"
1%		8"
0.3%		8.25"
0.3%		8.5"
0.1%		8.75"
0.1%		9"

= 1% of population
(note: 1 inch = 2.54 cm)

Average penis size, by population.

Perhaps, then, size doesn't matter. What we do know is that men are very attached to their willies. Except for those that aren't.

Vietnam veteran Alan Hall, 48, was spotted lurching in agony upon his front lawn next to his severed penis. Years before, Hall, of Fairfield, California, had been convicted of voluntary manslaughter in the death of Denise Denofrio. He told police that he had been seduced by a friend of hers who then sought a terrible revenge. In fact, Hall had used a hobby knife to mutilate himself. He asked police not to reveal the reasons why.

Other eye-watering stories have hit the news over recent years, sufficient to make castration appear the easy option. In New Zealand, student Thomas Hendry was determined to win the Trader McKendry's pub promotion entitled 'How far will you go?' He proved he had no limits when he stapled his penis to a crucifix, doused it with lighter fuel and set it alight. If that wasn't enough, he agreed to repeat the stunt for an American television station. Shockingly, footage of his penile pain was deemed suitable viewing by a New Zealand television watchdog. Meanwhile, shoplifter Barry Quemby received shocking injuries as he tried to shoplift a pair of live lobsters by thrusting them down his trousers. The 25-year-old had to be freed by police using pliers from the crustaceans' vice-like grip.

A Russian man who trapped his penis in a padlock had to be freed by Moscow firemen who used a saw on the lock after cold water and grease failed to secure his release. Afterwards the 20-year-old was told by doctors that his penis was fully functional but would now always be bent to one side. The man admitted he was forced to call the emergency services after a sex game went wrong.

And consider the plight of the policeman from Queensland, Australia, who was driving a rogue ferret from a town centre to the safety of a wildlife refuge in 2000, when it gnawed its way out of a box and bit the policeman on the penis. While remaining at the wheel – and you can't tell me that revenge wasn't the motive here – he subdued the feisty ferret with his baton.

If it isn't already obvious to you that penises should not be unduly meddled with, consider the cautionary tale of Walter Schmidt. Walter, from Munich, was tempted by the glossy advertisements for penis extensions and borrowed £5,000 from his mother to pay for the operation. The aim was to have three 76-mm (3-inch) extensions inside his appendage.

Alas, the wound left by the operation became infected, subjecting Walter to terrible pain. Then something went wrong with the inserts themselves, leaving Walter's penis disastrously altered. 'It's shaped like a triangle now, after one of the implants slipped down to the bottom. It's thick at the bottom and pointed at the top – and every time I put a condom on it falls off.'

Left on extended sick leave, with a penis that appeared shorter than ever and walking with a limp, Walter was seeking a refund of the operation costs so he could settle debts with his long-suffering mum.

In Tiflis, Russia, surgeons replaced one man's cancer-ridden penis with his finger, complete with knuckles. German papers reported that the 50-year-old man was able to go to the toilet normally within two weeks, through a tube inserted in the centre of the digit, which was amputated from the middle of his hand and attached to his groin in a 17-hour operation. It took a little longer before he used it as a sex organ, but the results were worth waiting for, according to the unnamed man's two girlfriends. The operation is to be patented and will be available at a cost of several thousand pounds.

Perhaps the penis's dilemma has been most aptly summed up by comedian Robin Williams who said: 'The problem is that God gives men a brain and a penis, and only enough blood to run one at a time.'

– CATA-LIST –

On average, one in eight Americans owns a cat.

There are 9 million domestic cats in the UK, compared with just over 7 million dogs. Meanwhile in America there are some 70 million cats shared among 34 million owners, against 58 million dogs.

We in the West are devoted to our feline friends. Keeping cats as pets has been a long-standing habit, with the most recent archaeological research claiming that wildcats, the ancestors of the modern cat, were kept domestically in the Stone Age almost 10,000 years ago. A skeleton of a cat was found in Cyprus recently, buried next to human remains dated at 9,500 years old, together with seashells and tools. The heads of human and cat were both pointing to the west, indicating a spiritual link between the burials. Poor puss was probably a sacrifice following the death of its owner.

Most Westerners will go out of their way to avoid harming a cat. Take Ian Green and Jon Gatiss who became concerned when they heard the pitiful mews of what they thought was a trapped cat in the kitchen of their home in Cheltenham, Gloucestershire, back in September 1998. First they called the fire brigade but nothing was found. Then the local inspector from the Royal Society for the Prevention of Cruelty to Animals came. Bill Dean even tried dangling a kipper below a raised floorboard, but it wasn't sufficient to tempt out the phantom cat. Finally an expert from the disaster relief charity Rapid UK came on the scene armed to the teeth with high-tech gadgetry. By now the kitchen was in pieces as the frantic home owners stepped up their search some nine days after first hearing the heart-wrenching cries. When John Holland got wired for sound, he finally identified the catcall – as the clock on the cooker.

A philosophical Mr Green said afterwards: 'If there is an animal trapped you have to do what it takes. They'd knocked the hell out of my house for a week and it was just a clock. But it had everyone fooled. It was a little cog whirring away in there and the noise was as cat-like as you can get. The funniest thing was that when we called out to the cat, it seemed to reply to us. It wouldn't make a noise for hours but when we shouted for it, there it was again.'

Given that the British are largely a nation of animal lovers, it is curious that car makers Ford and advertising agency Ogilvy & Mather should choose the decapitation of a cat to promote a new motor.

The advert showed a ginger puss climbing on a sleek, black car and peering through the sunroof. After the sunroof closes, the headless body is seen sliding down the car windscreen.

Ford was quick to point out that no animal was harmed in the making of the advert, which was made for Internet outlets but later rejected on grounds of bad taste. Somehow the clip was leaked and spread via email to a wide audience. More curious still, the ground-breaker in this advertisement series – which did win company approval – showed a pigeon being catapulted to its death by a car bonnet springing open.

– SQUARE-EYED MONSTERS –

American children spend about four hours a day watching TV.

Raconteur Noël Coward once said that television was for appearing on and not for watching. However, that nugget of wisdom has clearly bypassed subsequent generations that like nothing more than to park their butts in front of the television for hours...and hours...and hours.

According to the South Dakota department of health, the average American man spends 29 hours a week glued to the box. American women are worse, spending some 34 hours each week watching television; that's about five hours a day. In the USA small children are believed to spend an average of four hours a day viewing their favourite programmes, although the figure is slightly less among older children.

The American Academy of Pediatrics recommends that young children should watch television for no more than two hours per day – and that toddlers under the age of two should watch no television at all. The suggested limit for adults stands at ten hours a week.

Campaigners who want to see kiddies off the couch put forward studies that show that for each daily two-hour slot spent watching television, there is a 23 per cent increase in obesity and a 14 per cent increase in the risk for Type 2 diabetes. That's because TV gawpers get no exercise in those two hours – at all. Indeed, the remote control is more active than they are. More than that, they can still consume calories although they are expending none, as they are likely to sit and snack. If they were out and about the temptation to eat would decline.

– COUCH SLOUCHES –

Nearly nine out of ten British children stay indoors for almost the whole weekend.

The British can't afford to be smug on such issues either. Research carried out on behalf of the government has discovered that two-thirds of the UK population fall into a category nominally known as 'couch potatoes'. This means they do 'very little sporting activity at all'. Equally galling is the fact that a quarter of the population are branded 'cultural slouches' because they do very little of anything at all. A mere 5 per cent admits to going to plays, the opera, stately homes and museums.

Researchers deemed that watching sport and films could just about be counted as a cultural pursuit, and more than half the population were subsequently bracketed together as 'cultural consumers', albeit lowbrow in character. The overall picture is that Britain is a nation of observers rather than participants.

Sports minister Richard Caborn commented: 'We are a nation obsessed with sport, but sadly, as this survey shows, our obsession does not get enough of us off the couch and into the sports hall. With obesity levels dangerously high – 21 per cent of men and 24 per cent of women are now obese – it is time people realised they must change the way they live their lives.'

The study of 10,000 people was carried out by academics for the Department for Culture, Media and Sport. It may surprise some readers that there are substantially more women couch potatoes than there are men. About 71 per cent of women aged between 25 and 44 had little or no pursuits that took them off the sofa and into the great outdoors. That's about 15 per cent higher than for men. Report author Patrick Sturgis, a sociologist at Surrey University, said: 'The report reinforces the now familiar picture of sedentary Britain. The majority of people in the UK simply aren't engaging in the sort of activities that are essential to a healthy lifestyle.'

Another set of research carried out on behalf of the Early Learning Centre, a chain of toy shops, discovered that nearly nine out of ten British pre-schoolers spend most of the weekend indoors, in front of a screen. Six in ten children admit to watching TV four hours a day at the weekend. Three out of four parents admitted to using the television as a way of keeping their children occupied.

– IT'S A WONDERFUL LIFE –

Average life expectancy in America is on the up, standing at just under 77 years.

In the millennium year, the gap between women's and men's life expectancy was dropping, and likewise a traditional gap between white and black people was shrinking (women and whites being the most long lived). Given that at the turn of the 20th century, life expectancy at birth was a mere 47.3 years, while in 1950 it was 71.1 years for women and 65.6 years for men, it's obvious that great strides have been made in mortality rates.

All of this is a cause for celebration, you may think. But in fact there are some startling averages out there which put the US figures into sharp focus, the most crucial of which being the life expectancy figures for neighbouring Canada.

The average life expectancy for a Canadian woman is now 81.2 years, against 78.9 years for her American counterpart. Canadian men are likely to notch up 75.2 years while in America the figure is only 72.5 years. Indeed, there are 18 countries with populations of one million or more that have life expectancies greater than that of the USA.

An official report puts it all into context and warns against complacency. 'Childhood vaccinations are at the highest levels ever recorded in the United States. Fewer teenagers are becoming parents. Overall, alcohol, tobacco and illicit drug use is levelling off. Death rates for coronary heart disease and strokes have declined. Significant advances have been made in the diagnosis and treatment of cancer and in reducing unintentional injuries.

'But we still have a long way to go. Diabetes and other chronic conditions continue to present a serious obstacle to public health. Violence and abusive behavior continue to ravage homes and communities across the country. Mental disorders continue to go undiagnosed and untreated. Obesity in adults has increased 50 per cent over the past two decades. Nearly 40 per cent of adults engage in no leisure time physical activity. Smoking among adolescents has increased in the past decade. And HIV/AIDS remains a serious health problem, now disproportionately affecting women and communities of color.'

– ELITE EATS –

Once bread used to be cooked in ovens that didn't benefit from shelves and so the bread was always burnt on the bottom. It was customary to give workers or servants the bottom section while the resident family enjoyed the middle part. The best bit, the upper crust, was allocated to guests who were given special status. Soon those who were lauded and spoilt were described as 'upper crust'. The most pleasing aspect of this story is that the working classes were never once dubbed 'crusty bottom'.

– WALKING NOT SO TALL –

The average American man stands 1.77 metres (5'10") tall.

Although the life expectancy of Americans is going up, their average height is going down in comparison with their counterparts in Europe.

At the time of the American Revolution, the US soldier was on average 50 mm (2 inches) taller than fighting men from Britain. Now British men are 17.5 mm (0.5 inches) taller, while the Dutch – Europe's tallest people – can expect to look down on the Americans with their 50-mm (2-inch) height advantage. During the First World War, the average American soldier was 50 mm (2 inches) taller than the average German. But during the '50s, the height of the Americans appeared to be pegged while Europeans carried on growing. The average height of American men has actually slightly fallen in recent years.

Why then are the brakes going on American men's growth at around the 1.77 metre (5'10") mark? John Komlos of Munich University, who carried out the research in American and European physiques, believes unemployment, poverty and a diet of junk food are important factors. 'In Europe there is – in most countries – good health service provision for most members of society and plenty of protein in most people's diets. As a result, children do not suffer illnesses that would blight their growth or suffer problems of malnutrition. For that reason we have continued to grow and grow.'

The height of American women is also on a downward curve. According to the US Department of Health and Human Services, the average woman now stands at 1.62 metres (5' 3.7") and weighs 69 kg (152 lb). This is something less than 25 mm (1 inch) shorter than she was in the latter half of the 20th century.

Snide comments about junk food and its negative effects on the nation's health have not been lost on one of its most famous purveyors: McDonald's. Mounting a fight-back that has included salad, fresh fruit and bottled water, the giant corporation is even giving away a pedometer with every adult boxed meal in America and hopes to do so in Europe too. This device would measure the distance walked by the wearer and the number of calories used during such exercise. Health campaigners immediately retorted that it would take five and a half hours of walking to burn off the calories taken aboard with a typical McDonald's burger meal. (That's a Big Mac, large fries, large cola and McFlurry ice cream with candy, which adds up to a walloping 1,458 calories.)

Any health initiative is, of course, to be warmly welcomed. However, McDonald's latest bout of artery awareness came too late for its chief executive Jim Cantalupo, a former vice-chairman and president of the corporation, who died of a suspected heart attack in April 2004, aged 60.

– HEAD AND SHOULDERS ABOVE THE REST –

The average 1.82-metre (6-foot) worker earns $166,000 more than his 1.65-metre (5'5") counterpart during a 30-year period.

The stature scandal could have traumatizing effects on American men who for years have taken comfort in a succession of studies that have flagged up the advantages of being tall.

Tall people get married sooner, are promoted swiftly and can expert higher wages than their stubby colleagues. You can reap the rewards of being lofty early on, too, according to a report filed back in the '60s, which found that the tallest boys in the class were those most likely to get the first dates.

One study discovered that tall men earned more, although that was conducted in the good old days before Americans began to shrink.

Vertically-challenged Americans might take comfort from the words of Shawn Bradley, the 2.28-metre (7'6") tall center for the Dallas Mavericks, who has spent his life looking at the grubby places most of us will never see.

'I remember in high school…I could see over the top of all the lockers and it was disgusting: it was dusty, and there were empty drink bottles and articles of clothing that had been discarded up there and were lost forever. And my coach, who was about 6'4" (1.93 metres), stood on one of the benches so we could see eye to eye. He said: "You live in a dirty world, don't you?"

'Even in people's homes, if I have to duck through the doorway, there's dust on top of the molding. The tops of fridges are never clean.' But at least he looked in the right place for love. Shawn married a woman who stood just 1.60 metres (5'3") tall.

Sultan Koese, 22, probably the world's tallest man, tried issuing a Valentine's Day appeal for romance when he could see no prospect of a partner coming his way. Sultan – who is 2.41 metres (7'11") tall – has to convince first a woman, then her family, to accept him. 'Whenever relatives see me they don't want their daughters to marry me any more,' he admitted ruefully. Sultan, who lives in a small Turkish village, grew to his current dimensions after hormone treatment given in childhood went wrong. At the age of 19 he underwent surgery to stop him growing even taller.

– GUT REACTION –

Almost one-third of Americans are obese.

What the average American is missing in height he makes up for in girth. Almost one-third of adult Americans are classified as obese, according to 2002 statistics gathered by the National Health and Nutrition Examination Survey. To put it another way, no fewer than 59 million US bodies are blobby. More adult women than men are carrying the extra pounds. (That's 33 per cent of women and 28 per cent of men.)

It's a similar story among younger people. About 15 per cent of children and teenagers aged between six and 19 are overweight, about 9 million youngsters in total. More demoralising still, more than 10 per cent of very young children are too heavy to be healthy.

Obesity is something of a modern affliction. Figures taken by the NHANES in 1980 revealed there was little by way of a change in the size of the average American over the previous 20 years. But in the subsequent decade, figures leapt by a half – and the curve on the graph has kept going up and up. In a nation that munched its way through about 8.2 billion burgers in commercial restaurants in 2001, there's no respite in sight.

Fat is a costly business in the USA, as a couple of researchers deduced in 1998. The total burden on the national economy amounted to $51.6 billion in direct costs and a further $47.6 billion in indirect costs as they priced up numerous factors, including the number of lost workdays (39.3 million) and the number of visits to the doctor (62.7 million).

Consequently, the USA is the home of the fat camp, a diet-and-exercise summer break for children with weight issues. Alas, latest headlines imply that results achieved at fat camp will amount to nothing unless entire families change their lifestyles.

It might help to address the pain of being big though. There's not only the likelihood of being teased by peers and family members, but also the sad, complex phenomena revealed by one study recently. Researchers found that overweight adolescents claim to have more friends than they actually have. Or perhaps other children were reluctant to admit to having a friendship with someone who is overweight. Neither scenario is terribly appealing.

Given the American tendency to eat big, it is not surprising to find the ludicrous extravagance of a $1,000 (£565) omelette for sale in a New York hotel. Appearing on the menu as a 'Zillion Dollar Frittata', it contains 300 g (10 oz) of caviar, lobster and chopped chives.

On the first day it was available, no one bought it.

– WAISTING AWAY –

The average Briton eats £140 worth of crisps and sweets a year.

It's not just the Americans who are living it large these days. Needless to say, the trend for eating more and getting big because of it has drifted across the Atlantic to Britain, as a host of statistics will prove.

In just over 20 years, the number of obese British men and women rose from 8 and 6 per cent respectively to 22 per cent of the population. Among toddlers aged between two and four years, the rate of obesity surged from 5 to 9 per cent, while it trebled among those aged between six and 15.

The shock statistics are in a heavyweight report produced by the combined might of the Royal College of Physicians, the Faculty of Public Health and the Royal College of Paediatrics and Child Health. Sian Griffiths, president of the Faculty of Public Health, said: 'We are getting fatter because we are not taking enough physical activity and we are eating the wrong foods. Too many children are taken to school by car and too few ride their bicycles.'

The answer lies in part with the national diet. The average Briton tucks into £140 worth of crisps and sweets a year, making the UK the biggest nation of snackers in Europe. So says market analysts Datamonitor, blaming busy lifestyles for the increased tendency to eat between meals.

Choice of food is also crucial. Fifteen-year-old Craig Flatman eats nothing but jam sandwiches made with white bread, followed by a piece of chocolate cake washed down with two pints of semi-skimmed milk. At 1.85 metres (6'1") tall and weighing 70 kg (154 lb) his growth has not been impaired. Nor is his bizarre diet a matter of choice. Since babyhood, he has vomited when he has swallowed meat, fish, vegetables and fruit.

'I begin to feel sick if I put anything else into my mouth. It is a shame because I would love to eat things like burgers and chips,' says Craig, of Stowmarket, Suffolk. So at least he has a good excuse.

Whatever the reason, women's waistlines are soaring in size. Today's 11-year-olds are expected to possess a waist measuring 50 mm (2 inches) more than the average woman of 60 years ago. Data compiled by the Child Growth Foundation reveals just how young girls are blossoming. Standard patterns used by Marks & Spencer in the 1940s were cut to fit a woman measuring 33-21-33. Now the average waist size of an 11-year-old is just under 584 mm (23 inches) and rises to 610 mm (24 inches) for 13-year-olds. Meanwhile women's vital statistics today come in at 36-28-38.

Boys, too, are getting bigger than ever before. In 1954 the largest collar size in John Lewis's boys' shirts section was a 14. Today it has increased to a 17, while sweaters measure up to a 1.11-metre (44") chest size, when once 914 mm (36") was considered ample.

Concern about the rising size of children continues to mount. British doctors predict that one in three children will be seriously overweight by 2020 unless there are radical changes now in the content of the Western diet and the levels of inactivity that are symptomatic of today's young lifestyles. That means shedloads of heart problems and Type 2 diabetes.

Alistair Knox, senior lecturer in fashion at Nottingham Trent University and a contributor to the national sizing survey which obtains figures from shops, affirms that it is not just children who are getting bigger. 'We are all getting heavier, at the rate of around an extra pound a year.'

– TASTE OF INDIA –

Two-thirds of all meals eaten outside the home in Britain are curries.

There's no question that the British diet has changed beyond recognition, not least in a relatively new-found love of curry.

Believe it or not, commercial curry powder has been a feature of life in Britain since 1780 – a product of the lucrative spice trade that began centuries before – and the country's first curry house opened its doors in 1809 in London's Portman Square. However, it was following an influx of people from India, Pakistan, Bangladesh (as it became known) and Sri Lanka after about 1950 that curry was indelibly inscribed onto the national menu...so much so that chicken tikka masala is recognised as Britain's favourite dish.

According to figures from the Food Standards Agency, the Indian food industry in the UK is worth a cool £3.2 billion. London alone boasts more Indian restaurants than both Bombay and Delhi.

There are about 9,000 curry restaurants in the UK, employing about 70,000 staff, the largest concentration being in the West Midlands, Yorkshire, Scotland and South London, which together account for a quarter of all outlets.

The Brits in turn have made their mark on Indian cuisine. Chicken tikka masala is believed to have originated in Britain, after an Indian chef accommodated the British preference for moist food by adding tomato and onion paste to the traditional grilled chicken. Thanks to the unnamed hero, 1.1 million packets of the popular dish are sold in one single leading supermarket each year.

The French, on the other hand, have not taken to curry in the same way. Nothing like it, in fact, as culinary missionary Peter Farrell discovered to his cost. Documentary-maker Farrell could see the possibilities when he renovated a ramshackle property in southern France. He teamed up with pal Nippi Singh to buy a property in the hilltop idyll of Les Fabres, where both rued the lack of a decent local curry house.

But while Singh warned against a further venture, Farrell sought the input of a leading Indian restaurateur and decided to open an ethnic eatery in the charming village of Laurac. The trials and tribulations he experienced were captured on film in a popular reality TV series called *A Place In France*.

'There are Indian restaurants in the cosmopolitan centres and we thought there was a mood afoot for the French to be more adventurous in their cuisine.

'But they're not. As soon as winter came they retreated back to their meat and two veg regime and the whole thing went pear-shaped. Some days we didn't get anyone in at all.'

Farrell has been forced to sell the house he initially renovated with Singh to pay off debts. With typical British resolve, he has vowed to open a bed and breakfast for British tourists to the region, all within view of the cameras of course.

– ALL SHOOK UP –

Sometimes couples claim that the earth moves for them during sex. Not surprising, given the number of earthquakes that occur each year.

Most of us are only aware of the big ones, the tremors that bring down houses as if they were a pack of cards, cause multiple casualties and erase entire cities. Thank goodness those are the rare ones. The US Geological Survey estimates that earthquakes occur every year by the million. Most go undetected because they happen in remote areas or are so small that they don't even calibrate on the relevant machinery.

– EAST, WEST, HOME'S BEST –

Only 11 per cent of US citizens hold a passport.

But occasionally they do travel outside US borders. By an odd statistical quirk, the same number of Americans celebrated the millennium year by visiting Brazil as went to Taiwan. In figures released by the US Department of Commerce, these two countries were jointly the 16th most popular place for America's international travellers, attracting 671,000 US visitors apiece. Six countries tied for 20th spot that year, all beckoning 457,000 Americans. The half-dozen in question were the Philippines, Belgium, Greece, India, New Zealand and Singapore. However, those who know that even the boldest, most outgoing Americans tend to stay close to home will not be surprised to learn that the top two destinations for American tourists were its immediate neighbours, Mexico and Canada, attracting 18,849,000 and 15,114,000 US citizens respectively.

However, the urge to travel affects us all at some time, and even our garden ornaments are not immune. In the past 20 years there have been numerous examples of garden gnomes going walkabout in America, Europe and Australia. The first documented occurrence is believed to have been in Sydney, Australia, in the mid-1980s. The gnome-owners quickly received a postcard purporting to be from the absent ornament on vacation in Queensland. He returned two weeks later bearing a tan, which later was revealed to be brown shoe polish.

Barbara Austin, of Greensboro, North Carolina, was left a note when one of her three gnomes vanished that simply read: 'Gone travelin'. Back later.' And indeed, he did travel in the 50 days he was away, covering some 17,700 km (11,000 miles) through 28 states, into both Canada and Mexico. When he returned he brought with him a map and a photo album of him at landmarks, with friends, alongside art works and waiting in airport lounges. His companions were four men and a woman who occasionally featured in the snaps, like the rear view of man and gnome gazing across a city skyline. 'They're both just looking out over the city, wherever this city is, kind of daydreaming. For some reason it really strikes me,' says Austin.

Much of the charm of gnome-napping was dispelled by the radical French group 'Front de Libération des Nains de Jardin' or 'Garden Gnome Liberation Front'. This group claimed to have freed some 6,000 in the months after it launched in 1997. Many were returned to the forest where they were found in clusters, trying to return to their 'roots'.

Sometimes the endgame was altogether more sinister. Eleven garden gnomes were found hanged from a bridge in the village of Briey in France in 1998. A suicide note found at the scene said the intention was to 'quit this world' and go join a 'sect of the temple of submissive dwarfs'. A cell of the Garden Gnome Liberation Front, since disbanded, was believed to be behind the carnage.

Gnome travel was a feature of the popular French film *Amelie*, released in 2001, as the title character tries to induce her father to extend his horizons by dispatching his gnome on a world tour. Yet it failed to adequately highlight the plight of the gnomeless.

– ALL ARE BORED! –

More than a million Britons choose a cruising holiday every year.

Britons are again illustrating the subliminal urges of an island race by taking more cruises than ever before.

Once a holiday aboard a luxury liner was the preserve of the moneyed few who owned more than one tuxedo and had an intimate knowledge of cocktails and quoits. Recently reduced prices, brought about by bigger-than-ever ships, mean that this type of holiday has suddenly fallen within the reach of many more people, some whose only previous experience on the water is a rowing boat on the Serpentine.

The Passenger Shipping Association revealed that no fewer than 1,053,727 Britons enjoyed a total of 963,5800 cruises in 2003, a hefty 17.5 per cent increase on the previous year, while in 1992 the number of cruises enjoyed by Britons stood at just 229,000. It's now a £1 billion industry, to the delight of ship owners, specialist travel agents and the tat shops and brothel owners in ports worldwide.

Martin Tanner, a marketing manager with UK travel agency Cruise Control, said: 'Everybody thinks cruising is for old people, there's nothing to do and it's really expensive – that all people do is swan around in dinner suits at cocktail parties or sit in deckchairs with blankets over their legs watching the scenery go by when they're not playing bridge or shuffleboard.

'What's happened is that people are waking up to the new age of cruising – a floating resort with far more facilities than you can ever imagine in a land-based hotel. You've got some ships with an ice-skating rink, 5 swimming pools, 12 bars, 9 restaurants, a shopping mall, Jacuzzi, golf course...and this is all on a ship.'

But it isn't always plain sailing. Nine passengers ended up with green hair after taking the plunge in one cruise ship's pool. Those with fair or dyed hair appeared to be the worst affected on the P & O ship *Oceana*. Although levels of chlorine in the water appeared to be fine, the pool was drained and refilled as a precaution. Those left sporting an alien coiffure were referred to the on-board hair salon for treatment to rectify the cosmic colouring.

– WAY TO GO –

About 46,300 people die each week in America.

As we've said already, there are only two certainties in life: death and taxes. Well, some people can evade taxes. But nobody can sidestep death, as the 2,406,000 Americans who died by October of 2001 would have testified – if only they could.

Heart disease and cancer are the primary causes of death in America. But there are other ways of exiting, as headlines will tell us.

There was the 22–year-old would-be bungee jumper at Lake Accotink Park in Fairfax County, Virginia, in the summer of 1997: a fast-food worker who joined together bungee cords for his planned 21-metre (70-foot) fall from a trestle. Alas, he miscalculated and perished as he hit a pavement beneath his perch headfirst. A police spokesman said: 'The stretched length of the cord that he had assembled was greater than the distance between the trestle and the ground.'

He was an intellectual match for the Californian who feared his view of a predicted meteor shower during 1999 was inhibited by a nearby street lamp. So he forced open a hatch at the lamp's base and got to work with a pair of pliers. He was killed instantly by a shock from the 4,000-volt power cord.

Maxine Ann Keggerreis, 79, believed she could mow her lawn and exercise the dog at the same time in October 1997 – until the dog lead became entangled with the ride-on mower, pitching both dog and owner into a pond, where both drowned.

The 31-year-old user of a jet-propelled water bike on a lake north of Fort Lauderdale, Florida, in 2001 could not have known his assassin was about to swoop. The silent killer was a flying duck whose body was found floating near that of the biker, dead after receiving a blow to the head.

In Britain about 530,000 people die every year, according to the Office for National Statistics, fewer than half in a hospital bed. Young men aged between 20 and 44 are most likely to die in a car or a motorbike accident, while for women disease is the more potent threat. Then there are the deaths that nobody expects, like the 600 or so fatal injuries that occur every year on the stairs.

– NO, SIR, I DON'T MEAN MAYBE... –

Thankfully, baths and running water are common to most households these days. But cast your mind back not that many years and you will remember that homes were rarely graced with a tub. Washing was a bi-monthly event that took place in a freestanding bucket-style receptacle placed outside in the summer or in front of the fire in winter. It was hand-filled with water ready for the man of the house and he was followed in by his sons. Then it was the turn of the womenfolk, and only after mother and other daughters had lathered up and left would it be the turn of the baby. At this stage the water was distinctly murky and the prospect of throwing the baby out with the bathwater after the bath was carted off and upturned was not such a ridiculous one. So the phrase involving babies, bathwater and pointless exercises came into being.

– JUST VISITING –

Immigration and drugs control is a tall order in the USA. You can see why US customs officers practise those cold, hard stares when statistics show that each year 60 million people arrive on more than 675,000 commercial and private flights. Another 370 million come in by land and 6 million by sea. Around 116 million vehicles cross the land borders with Canada and Mexico, and more than 90,000 merchant and passenger ships unload 9 million shipping containers and 400 million tonnes of cargo at seaports. Not to mention the 157,000 small vessels visiting the harbours of coastal towns.

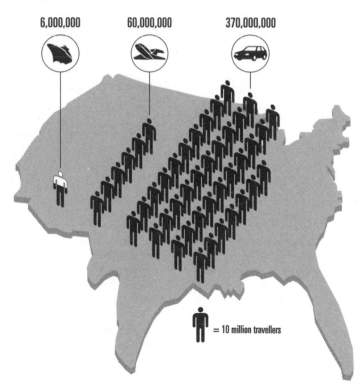

6,000,000   60,000,000   370,000,000

= 10 million travellers

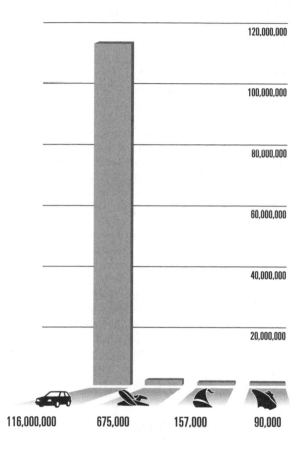

Above: The different modes of transport used to enter the US each year.

Right: How many travellers arrive in the US each year.

– WHAT'S THE WORST THAT CAN HAPPEN? –

On average, condoms are 98 per cent effective when they are used properly.

This, according to the Sexuality Information and Education Council of the USA. The quality of today's condom is better than ever before. That's partly because these days it is regarded as a medical device and, as such, comes under the stringent controls of the US Food and Drug Administration. Condoms are mostly made from latex, tapped from a rubber tree. Once each is made it is tested for pinholes, water leakage and must be able to hold 16 litres (4 gallons) of air without bursting.

All nervous teenagers who blow up condoms given out in sex lessons as if they were balloons should know that the idea has been thought of before. Still, condoms are a source of fascination and it is not unusual for the young to be curious about life, the universe...and sex. That's why the condom machine in the cinema toilet in the Austrian town of Braunau was like a magnet for 11-year-old Michael Steiner. What the youngster hadn't bargained for as he exercised his natural curiosity was getting his fingers firmly wedged in the machine.

A woman employee at the cinema was the first person who tried to rescue him. When she failed she called on the services of a nearby doctor. But red-faced Michael remained stuck fast until the local fire fighters dashed to the cinema with sirens and flashing lights. Only when they cut the vending machine into pieces was Michael released. He left with only cinema staff, the audience and the town's fire crews knowing his guilty secret.

– HAPPY RETURNS –

Andrew Robert Neil celebrates his birthday on 11 July, as does his father David Neil and grandfather Robert Lambie. A chance in a million, you might think. Not so, says a statistician from St Andrew's University. 'The chances are 160,000 to one. This happens approximately once in every two years in Scotland.'

– SILLY BUSTARDS –

According to the Royal Society for the Protection of Birds, 38 per cent of all bird species in Europe are considered at risk.

Another RSPB estimate says that 94 per cent of all birds that ever existed arc now extinct, with more than 80 species vanishing since 1600. Sometimes the figures are guess-timates, as colonies of birds – especially the small, brown, thoroughly indistinct varieties – pop up years after everyone thought they were goners. But it's easy to bring to mind birds that are no more, including the dodo, the great auk and the moa. There are greater efforts than ever before being channelled into saving our feathered friends, hampered sometimes by a general lack of acuity on behalf of the birds themselves.

Since the iron curtain came down in the '90s, levels of co-operation between Britain and Russia have reached new heights, not least in the realms of conservation. As a consequence, the great bustard, the world's heaviest bird, is about to make a return to Britain after an absence of almost 200 years.

The great bustard – which grows to nearly a metre (3 feet) in height and has a wing span of 2.06 metres (7 feet) – still roams freely on the Russian steppes, although its population worldwide is dwindling.

Eggs have been collected from nests in the wild, to be hatched in incubators as part of a joint British-Russian project. Up to 40 chicks will be flown to Britain to be released somewhere on Salisbury Plain where the birds were once a dinner-time delicacy served up to the mayors of Salisbury. The last sighting of a great bustard in Britain was in 1832.

Key to the success of the project was not, as you might think, the temperature of the incubator, the fertility of the eggs or the suitability of Salisbury Plain. It was two glove puppets made to look like great bustard hens. It is essential for the young chicks to remain wary of the human beings who are 'mothering' them in their first two weeks of life. Consequently, carers cloaked in robes and a mask fed the young birds by way of a glove puppet so the birds would keep humans at arm's length. You can't help but think these creatures were easily fooled.

Bustards may well have something in common with a heron that kept swooping to steal fish and frogs from Jim Bull's pond in Newport, Isle of Wight, England. He splashed out on a £25 plastic decoy heron, intended to ward off the unwelcome visitor, but the model bought in 1998 was so lifelike that the visiting heron developed romantic feelings for it. Mr Bull realised his plans were thwarted when he looked out to see the live bird performing mating dances around its singularly non-responsive chosen partner.

Another bird that proved none too bright was a parrot called Ollie who had a brief taste of freedom when he escaped from the cage at his home in Barnes, south west London, in August 1997. But he soon found himself back behind bars after flying into the ventilation system of Wormwood Scrubs prison, a few miles' distance as the parrot flies. Ollie was cared for by a lifer until his owners were traced through his identity band. Poor Ollie was freed from jail, but back behind bars once more.

– ONCE BITTEN, TWICE SHY –

An average great white shark has 3,000 teeth.

The largest carnivorous fish in the world is the great white shark (*Carcharodon carcharias*), immortalised in the Peter Benchley novel *Jaws* (and the subsequent Steven Spielberg film) and feared like no other. It can be distinguished from the rest of the shark population by the way it pokes its nose up out of the water, perhaps scanning the horizon for potential prey.

A well-fed great white regularly weighs up to 3.17 tonnes (7,000 lb) and has something in the order of 3,000 teeth. One of the beasts netted off the coast of southern France in 1829 was 6.7 metres (22 feet) long and allegedly contained the remains of a headless man in a full suit of armour. At the moment, the biggest verified specimen was a 6.4-metre (21-foot) female caught off Cuba in 1945 that tipped the scales at 3.31 tonnes (7,303 lb). Shark pups are often more than 1.5 metres (5 feet) long at birth.

The scent of blood attracts a great white and it can detect just one drop of the red stuff in 100 litres (25 gallons) of water.

There are about 100 shark attacks a year, and between 30 and 50 are carried out by a great white. These usually result in between 10 and 15 fatalities. Incredibly, there are people who live to tell the tale.

Like electrician Rodney Orr, who was snapped up by a great white in the Pacific near Santa Rosa, California, as he prepared to go spearfishing.

'He had hold of my head. I was at a right angle to its mouth, hanging out the side. The front teeth were buried in through my cheekbones and my nose. It was quick and sharp. The teeth were like razors. When he clamped on to me, it was a God-awful crunch. I heard the crunching and the teeth plough through the bone but it didn't hurt. Something in the brain clicks so you don't feel it till later.'

After Orr fought for his life, the shark released him. 'He had a hold of me for eight to 12 seconds. We probably travelled about 18–21 metres (60–70 feet).' Incredibly, despite leaving a trail of blood, he managed to get back to his paddleboard and escape to shore. After being helicoptered to hospital, he had about 80 stitches in wounds on his face, head and neck.

Latest research indicates it is unlikely that sharks mistake humans for seals, a primary food source. Great whites roar up to seals with zeal and tear them to shreds, whereas they tend to take a more leisurely approach with humans and are probably just exerting their curiosity. Bony humans are likely to clog up a shark's delicate digestive tract, so people are not a food they would choose.

Great whites have recently been the subject of a makeover, mostly thanks to Ralph Collier, president of the Shark Research Committee in California and author of *Shark Attacks Of The 20th Century*, who looks at averages in a different way.

He points out that during the 20th century there were 108 authenticated, unprovoked shark attacks along the Pacific Coast of the United States, of which eight were fatal.

'When you consider the number of people in the water during that 100-year period, you realise deadly strikes are very rare,' he says.

In his analysis of 20th-century shark data, Collier discovered that most attacks happened at the weekend during the months of August, September and October.

– SEE YOU LATER... –

There are an average of six alligator attacks in Florida every year.

Florida has an estimated one million alligators in residence. That same green corner of America attracts a vast number of visitors, some of whom like it so much they stay there forever. Alligators and humans don't make great bedfellows and that explains the annual rate of 12,000 complaints made about gators in Florida each year.

Surprisingly, the tenor of the complaints is not normally the vicious nature of alligators. Usually it is just that the snouty, savage, scaly reptiles have moved too close for comfort. The rate of alligator attacks in Florida averages at about six a year during the past 55 years, and out of a total of 326 attacks since 1948, only 13 have been fatal. The number of attacks appears to have increased in the past 15 years, according to the Florida Fish and Wildlife Conservation, either because more people than ever before live in Florida or an increased number of people are reporting alligator activity.

And if you think that being snapped up by an angry alligator means curtains, then you'd be wrong. Although female alligators often reach 2.8 metres (9 feet) in length and males several metres more than that, it is still possible to shake them off by putting up a fight. Alligators are avid but lazy in pursuit of food and are likely to let go of any potential dinner if it appears bigger and tougher than they are.

That's how 12-year-old Malcolm Locke survived when he was attacked by an alligator near his grandmother's home in Deltona, Florida, in the spring of 2004.

'It came right at me. First thing I noticed was its tail and then its mouth came right open. He bit my head and took a big chunk out of my ear,' explained Malcolm. With remarkable presence of mind he landed a punch on its nose – and that was enough to send the beast scurrying on its way. Although Malcolm will have to undergo plastic surgery on his injuries, his grandmother Linda Schlapper hit the nail on the head when she said: 'We're just lucky he's alive.'

– SUMER OF LOVE –

On average, one in every 3,400 Americans is an Elvis impersonator.

Hip-grinding, pelvis-thrusting, lip-quivering, eyelid fluttering, hair-quiffing, guitar plucking, hamburger-loving, pill popping, ever-living, cool fizzing Presley.

There has been no one quite like Elvis, before or since his death in 1977. The man was a phenomenon – so much so that he has sold more records than anyone else in record industry history. The number is one billion and rising.

Elvis has had 149 songs in Billboard's Hot 100 Pop Chart in America, of which 40 were in the top ten and 18 occupied the number one spot. More than 90 of his albums made the pop charts. And don't forget he was big in the R&B, country and gospel scenes, too.

Curiously, he won gold and platinum records in countries all over the world when he performed exclusively in North America. It is thought as much as 40 per cent of his total record sales took place outside the USA.

Stranger still is that he continues to inspire impersonators into hip swivelling and snarling, more than a quarter of a century after his death. American research has revealed that there are 85,000 Elvis impersonators at work in the States, compared with just 150 in 1977. One wit has pointed out that if the growth of Elvis impersonators continues at the same rate, one-third of the world will be at it by the year 2019. Fans – many of whom believe Elvis is still alive – have curious ways of expressing their own undying admiration. American Al Jacobs has drawn up a list of likenesses between the superstar and Jesus. He points out that Jesus once said: 'If any man thirst, let him come unto me, and drink.' (John 7:37) and Elvis said: 'The drinks are on me.' ('Jailhouse Rock' – 1957). Jesus said: 'Man shall not live by bread alone.'(Matthew 4:4). As for Elvis, well, he never ate bread on its own, but always with bananas and peanut butter. There are, by all accounts, two rival skydiving clubs for Elvis lookalikes, one of which being called 'The Flying Elvi'. Meanwhile in Britain, chef Mark Kemp sculpted a 910-mm (3-inch) high Elvis out of lard. The figure, fashioned in the kitchen of St Margaret's Hospice in Clydebank, Scotland, where he worked, had to remain refrigerated to prevent it from melting.

Still, one of the oddest tributes to Elvis comes from a Finnish professor and part-time crooner who translated 'Love Me Tender' into Latin. Plaudits rained down on the albums *Rocking In Latin* and *The Legend Lives Forever In Latin,* which included classics like 'Non Amare Non Possum' ('Can't Help Falling in Love') and 'Nunc Hic Aut Numquam' ('It's Now or Never'). It left Dr Jukka Ammondt hungry for more. And that's how he alighted on an even more obscure tongue than Latin to receive the Elvis treatment: Sumerian.

The Sumerians lived in 4000 BC in southern Mesopotamia and are best remembered for their superb craftsmanship in the city of Ur, in modern-day Iraq. Eventually eclipsed by Babylon, Ur was once the metropolis of the region and remained the hub of moon god worship. Sumerian language was preserved on tablets in cuneiform – wedge-shaped inscriptions – although no one knows how it was rightly pronounced.

When it came to translating the Carl Perkins song 'Blue Suede Shoes', made famous by Elvis, there were some obvious difficulties, not least that the Sumerians didn't have shoes, let alone pairs that were blue and suede. As a consequence, the hit song became 'Sandals of Sky Blue Leather'. Ammondt was ably assisted by Simo Parmola, professor of Assyrology at the University of Helsinki and Director of the State Archives of Assyria Project.

For the literally minded among you, the refrain goes like this: 'Nig-na-me si-ib-ak-ke-en, e-sir-kus-za-gin-gu ba-ra-tag-ge-en.'

Translation:
'On my sandals of sky-blue leather do not step.'

Ammondt has recorded the song with two others in Sumerian and performs live wearing a leather kilt, blue leather sandals and is backed by musicians in the garb of Sumerian governors.

He explained: 'There is a primitive strength in Sumerian and singing this language is like a holy ritual for me. I wish that this recording in Sumerian could bring us a message reminding us, people of the New Millennium, of the importance of those ancient cultures that are the basis of our modern lives.'

– HISS AND BOO SHOW –

*Every year more than 8,000 people are bitten by poison-
ous snakes in the USA.*

Fortunately, fewer than ten will die after shipping some
snake venom, so even if you feel the fangs you've still only
got a one in 800 chance of being a fatality. The flip side of
that amazing fact is that you have more chance of dying
from a bee or wasp sting than you do from a snake bite.

The most common poisonous snakes in America are
rattlesnakes, copperheads, coral snakes and cottonmouth
or water moccasin snakes, although it is rattlers that are
the worst offenders.

(Some helpful advice here should you come face to face
with an angry snake: if its pupil is round, then it's no
worries because it is non-poisonous. The venomous types
have elliptical pupils. See one and weep.)

Snake handler John Kenyon was bitten by a coral snake
during a show at the Billie Swamp Safari on the Big
Cypress Seminole Indian reservation, probably because he
had not washed thoroughly after previously feeding rats
and mice to his snakes.

'It didn't hurt, it was just a pinch or like someone had
grabbed my skin with a pair of pliers and pulled lightly.'

The show came to an abrupt halt as he was whisked off for
medical care. 'The pain didn't happen right away. When it
started to swell is when I felt the pain. It wasn't throbbing
exactly, but there was a burning sensation. The swelling
finally got up to my lymph nodes under my armpit, but the
intense part of the pain went up to my elbow. The doctors
originally wanted to raise my arm so the swelling would go
down but that would've sent the venom straight to my

heart.' Kenyon made a full recovery after treatment with anti-toxin.

Others are not so lucky, and those at risk include people who choose to handle the most poisonous types as a demonstration of their faith. Snake handlers are responding to a phrase in Mark's gospel, which in chapter 16, verses 17–18 says, concerning true believers, 'they shall take up serpents'.

Rev Dwayne Long, 45, died from a snakebite he suffered handling a rattlesnake during an Easter service at a church in Lee County, Virginia, one of an estimated 80 people who have died in similar circumstances during worship since the practice began at the beginning of the 1900s.

Snake stories often have an unhappy ending. A man who broke the world record for staying with snakes died after being bitten by a mamba. Boonreung Bauchan spent seven days in an enclosure with snakes in 1998 to claim a place in the Guinness Book of World Records. Five years later he was bitten after handling a snake he had recently captured in the jungle during a show for villagers in Thailand where he lived. He continued with his performance after taking a herbal medicine and a shot of whisky but collapsed soon afterwards. His father said that 30 snakes resident at his home would now be given to a zoo.

But just sometimes human beings get their revenge. South African Lucas Sibanda decided to turn the tables on the python that ambushed him as he walked home from work in Klingat, near Pretoria. Sibanda bit the snake just below the head and kicked and punched as the predator tried to get a grip. When the surprised snake finally gave up the fight, Sibanda killed it with a stick and dragged it home.

– FILM BINGES –

Spider-Man 2 smashed US box office records when it opened in July 2004, earning £22.26 million in its first day – or almost £950,000 per hour.

The next contender in the box office records stakes is the first *Spider-Man* movie, released in 2002, which coined £21.65 million on its first day. That's £900,000 per hour.

The cash came rolling in despite a number of continuity errors highlighted on the Moviemistakes website. At 33 blunders, the film was the third most mistake-ridden film of the year upon its release. Included are a miraculous repair in Spider-Man's mask and a scar on Peter Parker's cheek that switches between left and right. (This info is from the same website that claims a gas canister is seen in a chariot in *Gladiator*, but is rarely spotted by audiences.)

Yet as popular as many big budget movies are it is the unassuming, unlikely releases that tend to become long-term cult viewing – with exceptions like *The Sound Of Music* which has become a modern-day *Rocky Horror Picture Show*, with legions of movie-goers dressing in drag and singing along. More typical is *The Blues Brothers*, made in 1980, which bombed at the box office. Yet this comic car chase starring John Belushi and Dan Aykroyd spawned a stage show 20 years after its damp squib display in cinemas, and remains a rite of passage for petrol heads everywhere.

A more recent cult hit was *The Big Lebowski*, made in 1998 and starring Jeff Bridges and John Goodman. It's about an unprepossessing hero who calls himself The Dude and whose recreational pursuits are primarily bowling, drinking and smoking pot. It's about what happens when he gets mistaken for a rich bloke by kidnappers, but that is almost incidental. Its devotees revel in the oddball characters haunting the bowling alley that are by turns compelling, pitiful and downright awful. There are yearly Lebowski fests in the US, in which hundreds of fans dress like the characters, chant chunks of dialogue and sink White Russians, the chosen tipple of the hero.

But if drinking is your game, you should join fans of the cult hit *Withnail And I*, made in 1986 and starring Richard E Grant, Paul McGann and Richard Griffiths.

It's about two out-of-work London actors who visit the country and drink a lot. Film buffs are once again capable of quoting mighty portions of dialogue (with feeling) while ardent fans try to match the heroes drink for drink when watching the video.

If you want to buy in for a session with *Withnail And I*, take the following shopping list and line the drinks up before pressing play.

    One glass red wine
    One large glass gin
    One pint of cider
    One bottle of sherry
    One glass red wine
    Three glasses of whisky
    One glass of sherry
    One pint of beer
    One quadruple shot of whisky
    One pint of beer

> One glass of red wine
> One glass of Pernod
> One glass of red wine
> One glass of whisky
> One glass of red wine

Presumably the dialogue drones are defeated by copious consumption by, say, halfway through the film, so that's a blessing. The game doesn't carry a warning, but is obviously perilous to health.

A similarly dangerous drinking game has evolved from the *Inspector Morse* television series among Oxford University students. Essentially, it's a finger's depth of drink every time reference is made to a college or location that doesn't exist, whenever Morse patronises his sidekick Lewis, when Oxford University stereotypes are depicted on screen and each time Morse starts a sentence with the words 'Let's go through it again.'

You drink three fingers-worth when someone gets killed, when you see someone you recognise, after spotting scenery that is not in Oxford or its environs and when Morse explodes with the words: 'Good God, Lewis.'

And it's time to finish your drink entirely when the murderer is arrested, when Morse gets paranoid about Masonic links in the police force or society at large and whenever the time-worn detective makes a personal revelation.

– LIFE OF GRIME –

Three per cent of Britons never do housework.

Yet although some Brits have an aversion to cleanliness, they are still the most house-proud in Europe.

A Mintel survey carried out in 2004 revealed that 6 per cent of French people questioned admitted to doing no housework. Sixteen per cent of Spaniards never wield a duster in anger and a mighty 20 per cent of Germans – one in five – keep the broom firmly in the cupboard. (Do keep in mind, though, that the Germans were more likely to hire domestic cleaners than any other nation quizzed.)

One in five of the 25,000 Britons questioned said they spent 'a lot of time' cleaning. And, big surprise, it is women who are doing most of the mopping and polishing. More women are working than ever before while still strutting their stuff as domestic goddesses.

In total, four out of five British women spend a lot or a fair amount of time cleaning against just 52 per cent of men. Perhaps they are the authors of their own downfall as 70 per cent admitted to taking satisfaction in housework, compared with 47 per cent of men. It's the same story in Germany, France and Spain, at least among the 10,000 people questioned there. Typically the women do chores while the men do things less mundane.

Curiously the well-off in Britain cared least about the state of their homes. The highest earners in Britain were most likely to say that their house was often a mess.

– KISS THIS –

Ninety-seven per cent of women kiss with their eyes closed, against 37 per cent of men.

Those are the findings of a Canadian anthropologist who studied the smacker. We've all got our own theories as to why women shut their eyes, not least because a little imagination can go a long way when it comes to your average man. As for men, the actor Anthony Quinn believed they kept at least one eye open to ensure the wife was not approaching.

Kissing has long been an everyday feature of Western life, with the Romans adopting the routine on arrival home primarily to check who had been at the wine in their absence.

Historically it was less accepted in the orient and the Japanese responded badly when the nation was exposed to kissing – both pecks and full frontal snogging – with the onset of the age of cinema. In 1926 Tokyo's Prefect of Police cut some 244,00 metres (800,000 feet) from reels of imported American films to uphold the country's morals. Only after World War II were screen kisses deemed acceptable in Japan. Similarly, it was customary for Indian women to avert their gaze if a kiss occurred in the cinema until screen kissing became acceptable as late as 1977.

Meanwhile, the West was comparatively kissing away. A record was made when Jane Wyman and Regis Toomey kissed for a full three minutes and five seconds in *You're In The Army Now*, made in America in 1940.

But that's nothing to the kissing feat achieved by Alice Johnson, a 23-year-old waitress, who won a car in Santa Fe, America, in 1994 after kissing it for 32 hours and 20 minutes. There's no record of whether her eyes were open or closed, but she is known to have loosened four teeth in the process.

It's not as though everyone in the West approved of kissing, however. In 1909 the Anti-Kissing League was formed in the US by people who considered the practice unhealthy.

Kissing is generally accepted as a good thing these days. But that's not why the word appears on some sports equipment. When KISS is written boldly on bats and racquets, it is an acronym to reminder the user of one of the fundamental principles of competitive sport: Keep It Simple, Stupid.

– EAT, DRINK AND BE WARY –

There were some horrible habits in Ye Olde Englande and this is borne out by phrases still used today. During the Middle Ages, the flooring of the poorest households was made of earth, while posher accommodation enjoyed slates or tiles. That's how the phrase 'dirt poor' came into usage.

The poor were also rarely in a position to feed themselves meat. Only on special occasions were they able to 'bring home the bacon' and when it happened they hung it out for everyone to see. If they shared the prize, neighbours came around to 'chew the fat', presumably indulging with delight in the bits that today hit the slaughterhouse floor.

Worst of all, and hardest to believe, is the root of the funereal wake. Apparently, when copious amounts of alcohol were consumed from lead cups, the drinker could fall into a deep slumber that very much resembled death. After being laid out for burial, the family would gather round with drinks in hand to see if the 'victim' revived, the effects of a double dose of poisoning having worn off.

Allegedly, this became a habit after coffins were dug up for reuse and scratch marks discovered on the inside of the lids, made by those who were sent to meet their maker too soon.

– HARD TO STOMACH –

In every 30-minute cookery show made in Britain, America and Canada there are an average of seven food hygiene blunders.

Cookery is the new sex on television but, like all such pleasures, it comes with a high risk of disease.

Cleanliness errors abounded when the top TV chefs were scrutinised by a team of food scientists at the University of Guelph in Ontario, Canada, and some of them were pretty basic. In three-quarters of the programmes watched by the experts, there were examples of cooks failing to wash their hands. Ugh.

There were almost as many instances of raw and fresh foods being laid side by side. Another common mistake was to taste dishes from a spoon that is then used to add more ingredients. Well, we've all done that...haven't we?

Actually, we don't need to defend the chefs – none of whom were named and shamed by the way – because they weren't that bothered themselves.

Nigella Lawson said she took pride in her tough immune system, which probably evolved after a childhood spent eating her mother's hair in dishes. 'I agree that it is good to educate people, but it would be foolish to push it too far,' she said.

Anthony Worrall Thompson also played the immunity card, saying: 'This paranoia about hygiene is the downfall of modern society.'

We'll bear that in mind when we pay over the odds for a meal in a TV chef's restaurant then.

– JACKPOT JAPES –

UK lottery ticket sales are worth £88 million per week.

It's been a tough few years for Camelot, the company that runs Britain's National Lottery. Sales fell steadily from £100 million per week in the late 1990s to the present average of £88 million. Overall, ticket income did rise by 1 per cent to £4.6 billion in 2003, but analysts still talk of 'lottery fatigue' among the public.

How different it was back in December 1994 when Camelot announced that its first big jackpot winner had scooped £18 million. This was great news for the company, given its massive TV ad campaign showing a giant, sparkling hand descending from the heavens to point at 'ordinary' people. The accompanying slogan was: It Could Be You.

Newspapers were desperate both to name the lucky punter and dig some dirt on him. Unfortunately, to Camelot's chagrin, the man concerned had requested anonymity. Tabloid switchboards were soon inundated with tipsters convinced that a friend or relative had been acting strangely and was therefore unquestionably the lottery squillionaire.

Eventually, after a two-week manhunt, the *News Of The World* correctly fingered the winner as Mukhtar Mohidin, a 42-year-old father of three from Blackburn, Lancashire. Under the tag-line 'His name is Mukhtar. He dreamt of a corner shop. Now he's worth £18 million', the paper helpfully offered a potted family history.

The jewel in its coverage was a full-page picture onto which was scanned that familiar sparkling hand from the 'It Could Be You' TV ads. It was pointing straight at Mukhtar's mugshot and the headline was simple and masterful: 'IT WAS HIM.'

– A SENSE OF ENTITLEMENT –

UK lawyers working for a percentage of a compensation claim settlement take, on average, £40 for every £100.

That's according to a 2002 study by the insurer Norwich Union – which goes on to say that the average UK household pays £500 a year through insurance premiums and taxes to meet the nation's £10 billion bill for compensation claims.

The NU survey also highlighted some horrendous public hypocrisy: namely that while three-quarters of interviewees believed Britain's 'blame 'n' claim' culture was wrong, half said they were more likely to lodge claims. A staggering one in five said they would sue whenever they could.

It's not as though the lawyers have time on their hands. Not with clients like Nikolay Kozlov from Yekaterinburg, Russia, who in 2004 took his ex-girlfriend to court demanding she return the chocolates, nuts and fruit he gave her before she dumped him. In a letter to the Yekaterinburg judges his ex said she couldn't return the gifts – including six pounds of bananas, Swiss chocolates and 'a bright red apple' – because she'd eaten them.

And the compensation cases are becoming ever more bizarre. In March 2004 a 28-year-old Birmingham receptionist, Helen Terry, was paid a 'substantial sum' by local radio station BRMB as recompense for injuries suffered during its 'Coolest Seats In Town' contest. She had to sit on a block of dry ice for an hour in an attempt to win tickets for a Geri Halliwell concert. The ordeal caused permanent scarring on her bottom and legs together with third-degree burns from severe frostbite.

– MITE DODGY –

The average lifecycle of the cat ear mite is 21 days from egg to adult.

Cat ear mites lay an average of five eggs per day, usually on the lining of the ear canal. These hatch within four days, after which the larvae feed for a further four days on epithelial debris (look it up). They then moult into immature insects or 'nymphs', which in turn feed for three to five days to reach adult form. You won't be surprised to learn that a single ear can house several thousand, voraciously hungry mites.

It was quite brave then for Westport, NY vet Robert A. Lopez to conduct a series of cat ear mite experiments on himself. In 1994 he spent 11 weeks removing mites from cats and inserting them in his own lug holes to record their scratching, biting and eating habits. After suffering plenty of sleepless nights – and washing his ears out occasionally – he concluded that mite bites reach their height mainly after midnight and before 3am.

Lopez's work earned him an 'Ig Noble Award', a kind of anti-Nobel prize awarded annually by the US-based *Annals of Improbable Research* organisation. In accepting his prize, he offered the following ditty: 'I hate the old didactic mite. All he does is crawl and bite. At sleeping time he acts like a bum. And crawls right in to your ear-drum.'

Other Ig Noble winners include David Schmidt of the University of Massachusetts, for his theories on why shower curtains billow inward, and Yuri Struchkov of Moscow's Institute of Organoelemental Compounds, who between 1981 and 1990 published 948 scientific papers at an average of one every 3.9 days.

At least there was only one Yuri Struchkov. Spare a thought for readers checking the credits on a research paper published in the 2 September 1993 issue of *The New England Journal of Medicine*. Remarkably, it had 976 co-authors and therefore 100 times as many authors as pages.

– MEET THE PARENT –

On average, one in every 200 men alive today is descended from Genghis Khan.

The first billion on the planet was notched up in 1802 and it was 125 years later before the population doubled. However, during the 20th century humans began to mushroom, mostly due to declining death rates rather than booming birth rates. The third billion was reached in 1961, while ten years later the fourth was duly achieved. By 1987 there were five billion people living on the planet, with six billion reached in 1999 and seven billion scheduled to be living and breathing by 2010.

There are lots of spooky facts about world population, like that every 20 minutes it grows by 3,000, that its growth amounts to 76 million a year and that nearly 6 per cent of all the people who have ever lived are alive today.

But perhaps most astonishing of all is that 0.5 per cent of men alive in the world today – some 17 million or one in every 200 – are descendents of the Mongol marauder Genghis Khan.

At the time of his death in 1227 he had forged an empire stretching from Japan across Asia to the Caspian Sea. But he was a lover as well as a fighter, who took his pick from the most gorgeous beauties of the age.

Modern investigations of chromosomes and DNA and other things we can't explain in these columns point to a link. Suffice to say that most men in the last millennium have something in the order of 20 descendents alive today. Genghis Khan appears to have been a biological superman who passed on his strong genes in quantity. Next project on the blocks is to write his family tree.

– TRYING OUR LUCK –

The gross gambling revenue taken by American casinos increased by an average $1.69 billion a year between 1993 and 2002.

Global gambling is expanding at a phenomenal rate, driven by the rise in Internet casinos and a general relaxation of betting laws. As you'd expect, the USA is setting the pace, with gross gambling revenue (wagers minus winnings) from commercial casinos more than doubling in the ten years to 2002. When you add in all other forms of legal betting – horse-racing, online sports etc – Americans spend upwards of $650 billion annually. That's more than the nation's entire annual food bill.

Casinos have performed particularly strongly, as these figures from the American Gaming Association prove.

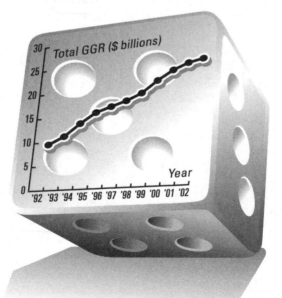

Year	Total GGR ($ billions)
1992	9.6
1993	11.2
1994	13.8
1995	16.0
1996	17.1
1997	18.2
1998	19.7
1999	22.2
2000	24.3
2001	25.7
2002	26.5

This is all the more remarkable when you consider that most US casinos market themselves both to poverty-line mothers pushing dimes into slot machines and the so-called 'whales', high-rolling millionaires playing the poker or roulette tables. Even among the whales there's a big betting league and, generally speaking, Kerry Packer is rarely far from the top of it.

The Australian media magnate, whose personal fortune stood at around AUS$3 billion in 2002, is something of a living legend among gamblers. Upmarket casinos don't discuss gains or losses openly, but all the indications are that during the 1990s, Packer took the Las Vegas MGM Grand for $26 million at blackjack, playing six hands at a time for $200,000 a hand.

The managers eventually suggested he should either play elsewhere or agree a cap on his stakes. Perhaps they should have held out longer, because in September 1999 the British tabloids reported a losing streak at London's Crockfords which cost him £11 million ($16.5m). The following year he was said to have kissed $20 million goodbye at the baccarat tables in US casino Bellagio.

Urban myth it may be, but the best Packer anecdote concerns the night he found himself in a Las Vegas casino alongside a pretty girl and a loud, boastful Texan. The girl was clearly unhappy with the oilman's crass chat-up lines and eventually Packer interrupted, asking him to repeat the extent of his personal wealth. The redneck eyed the Aussie upstart scornfully. '$100 million sir.' Packer thought for a moment. 'Tell you what,' he said, 'I'll toss you for it.' The offer was declined.

– SORRY SEEMS TO BE THE HARDEST WORD –

Sixty-five per cent of US children aged between two and 17 use the Internet from home or school.

Computer ownership is on the up as well, with 83 per cent of all American family households owning a computer in 2002, a rise of almost 20 per cent on figures from two years earlier.

The findings are from a report by the Corporation for Public Broadcasting in America which, not surprisingly, found that teenagers comprised the greatest number of users.

One hopes they are logging on to expand their general knowledge and assist their studies rather than to investigate some of the vile sites available on the Internet. In 2002 a study by the European Union found that a quarter of eight to 17 year olds found porn on the Net, sometimes by accident, sometimes on purpose. Britain's Department of Education and Skills recently discovered that 70 per cent of children over the age of ten had seen potentially harmful material while browsing through Internet pages. More than half of the children questioned spent more than five hours a week linked up to the Internet on their computer. Meanwhile, 80 per cent of parents did not know how to use security settings that could eliminate the crude, rude and vulgar.

But not to worry if you're caught looking up naughty sites – you can now use the same computer to make amends.

There's an apology site that has been a storming hit and, those with kids will be happy to know, it is jam-packed full of children saying sorry to parents.

It is the brainchild of author Jay Rayner who launched it to help publicise his novel called *The Apologist*, about a man who seeks to say sorry for every wrong thing he has ever done.

After appearing on day-time television in the UK, Rayner's site was swamped with contributions from people seeking to unburden themselves of weighty guilt, sometimes years after the event.

There are people who are genuinely sorry, like the person who confessed that he/she had thrown a little brother's pet rat out of the window after being bitten and watched as it was run over by a passing Mini Cooper. The rat's name was Frank, but clearly the perpetrator was not and felt the responsibility of the rat's death keenly and alone.

And contrite teenagers abound on this website with messages to mums and dads – some of them dead already – about youthful misdeeds. 'Mum, you always understand things about me and it's a shame I can't tell you some of the terrible things I have done without your permission and trust. I just want to say I'm sorry for going behind your back. I love you.'

Tear-jerking stuff, as are the messages to dead pets like that written to Flo, who used up her ninth life playing on the road. 'I miss you sooooooo much, you were more than just a pet, you were my little chum.' The email goes on in a similar vein from the heartbroken owner of this two-year-old feline.

There are a heap of apologies to teachers for playground pranks that obviously caused utter misery at the time. Spare a thought for the teacher who had glue smeared on his glasses – at least someone in the class has written an apology – and for the woman teacher who was hounded from her classroom into a cupboard by kids mocking her dress sense.

But a whole load more people write to say sorry when you are left with the distinct impression they are anything but. 'I'm so very sorry for having messed up three marriages and made each husband so miserable, especially my third husband with whom I had two children...well, actually, one wasn't his. I'm sorry for having screwed half of my home city including a brother-in-law.' The message goes on to reveal that the writer has moved to Australia with the intention of looking for a really rich man to attend to her whims. Not exactly in purgatory about her misdemeanours, then.

So if your teenager stands up after a session on the computer with a spring in his step and a tissue in his hand, let's hope this is the website he has been visiting.

– AGAINST ALL ODDS –

After being tossed, a coin is more likely to land the way it was facing when it started out.

Those are the findings of a coin flipping analysis carried out by three leading statisticians in America, who have cast doubt on the legitimacy of this time-honoured way of settling disputes.

'I don't care how vigorously you throw it, you can't toss a coin fairly,' said one of the statisticians, Persi Diaconis from Stanford University.

It was once assumed that chance really did play its part in coin-tossing, providing the coin span around a horizontal axis. Each throw was independent of the one that went before and the one that came afterwards. The probability of it landing as 'heads' was still 50 per cent, no matter if the throw happened after a string of 'tails'.

However, it's now believed a truly random throw is unlikely to occur because a coin sometimes wobbles rather than properly flips.

The margin, although relevant, is very small. Diaconis admitted that it would take 10,000 tosses before a bias became apparent. That's not the same of a coin spinning on its edge, which mostly frequently favours a particular direction because the imprints and reliefs on it subtly alter the rotation.

And then there's the story of the university professor who chose flipping a coin as a simple method to illustrate the conundrum of chance and probability. Dr Jeffery Hamilton from Warwick University tossed a 2p coin that spun, just as most coins do. However, unlike most other coins, this one came to rest on its edge, a feat that the lecturer could never hope to repeat. After a stunned silence, students who witnessed the event in October 1972 gave him a round of tumultuous applause.

If your head is left spinning by all this talk of random probability and statistics then spare a thought for the Hindu ascetic who is rolling bodily across the sub-continent as part of a quest for peace. Ludkan Baba – known as the rolling saint – is believed to have rolled barrel-style for thousands of miles during a 19-year spinning career.

He is a sadhu, a devotee seeking to release himself from the cycle of reincarnation that Hindus believe governs their existence. In the *Los Angeles Times* he is reported as saying: 'I move during cyclone, during blazing summers and cold winters. I think of God, I think of Mother Earth and then I roll and roll and roll. I don't feel dizzy. I don't consume any food, just tea and cigarettes. At night I eat fruits, roti [bread], whatever I can lay my hands on.' His mode of dress is the traditional *dhoti*, or loin cloth.

Bizarrely, he doesn't appear starved or battered by the close-quarter effects of rough terrain. However, he got used to tough living after he entered a cave in 1973 and stayed there for 12 years, living only on grass and water. His isolation came to an end when he received a divine message to start rolling for peace.

A mission in 2004 between his home in Madhya Pradesh to the Pakistan city of Lahore – a distance of some 2,400 km (1,500 miles) – to end hostilities in the disputed Kashmir region brought him to world attention. In fact, he has already achieved a 3,998-km (2,485-mile) long roll between his home town and the significant Hindu shrine of Vaishno Devi. Although traffic and well-wishers peg his pace to a sedate 9.6 kph (6 mph) he can reach up to 24 kph (15 mph) unhindered on the open road.

– SCREEN PETS –

After their debut in 1996, Tamagotchi digital pets sold 40 million units in their first two years.

You remember these hideous gadgets named for the Japanese term for lovable egg. They were small, hand-held monitors on key chains with vague representations of pets on the screen. The pets had to be fed and cleaned and exercised, all done at the touch of a button.

Very laudable too, as it taught children that all pets need regular care. But the irritating beeps that echoed incessantly around shopping malls drove all non-Tamagotchi keepers to distraction. And there was concern (in this household at least) as pre-teenage Tamagotchi owners took sadistic pleasure in killing off their pets in the worst way they could contrive. But if we were pleased to see the back of them before the dawn of the new millennium, then our elation has proved premature.

A new improved model was launched in the spring of 2004, promising better graphics although still film noir. Inevitably there will be cell phone links.

This time however the pet can evolve, will mate and can even have babies. The toy's makers, Bandai, have developed a way for one Tamagotchi to communicate with another. If the vibes are right then fireworks spark across the corresponding screens. Aaah.

Executives at Bandai doubt they can recreate the success of the original Tamagotchi, which became popular before the advent of numerous other high-tech toys. Yet they might be on to a winner as stressed, overly stretched people in the modern world find themselves unable to live lives normal enough to include a pet.

A company in Merseyside, Britain, has launched a virtual dog walking service that is patronised by owners too busy to take a trek with the pet themselves. Owners can, however, log on to the Internet to see other people walk their precious pooch – and pay for the privilege of doing so. The dog creche is doing a roaring trade. Presumably couples who can now park children and dogs with other people during daylight hours are rejoicing in all the freedom they now have.

– ONE OF US –

In a survey carried out by the Comic Buyer's Guide, *Batman was voted the most popular comic book hero of the last century.*

He's been around since 1939 when he made his first appearance in *Detect Comic* (No 27). Since then he has appeared on the small screen and in films as well. Batman, aka Bruce Wayne, and his sidekick Robin – along with dastardly foes like the Joker, the Riddler and the Penguin – is the stuff of childhood.

His creator was Bob Kane who was inspired by a Leonardo da Vinci sketch of a man trying to fly, a 1930s silent movie called *The Bat Whispers* and another film, *The Shadow and Zorro*. With the character comes the tragi-noble story of how a young Bruce saw his parents murdered and vowed from that day to fight crime. He uses his vast fortune to buy crime-busting gadgets, which helps to clean up the streets of Gotham City.

In 1995 Bob Kane commented on the enduring popularity of his creation. 'Batman is associated more with the average man than Superman. He doesn't have super-powers, but that's part of the longevity of him. He's Mr Average Guy. He could bleed and die. Couple that with the fact that he fights for the oppressed. He battles for everyone.'

Batman has obviously been an inspiration to many, including two oddball do-gooders from Middle England. When two football match streakers at Reading in Berkshire were brought down by two men dressed as Batman and Robin, the crowd roared its approval. Soon afterwards, the dynamic duo was back in action again and was by now attracting the attention of the local newspaper. An appeal for information by journalists revealed that the superheroes had been spotted in the shops at Whitley in Berkshire, presumably warding off muggers. On another occasion they also pushed Michelle Kirby's car to a petrol station after it ran out of fuel. She said later: 'They just appeared. I saw them running down the road in Batman and Robin outfits – I was laughing so much.

'They said "I'm Batman, I'm Robin", and I said "No, you're not." I asked them if they were going to a fancy dress party, but they said they were going back to Gotham City.'

– PORKY PIES AND ALIBIS –

About 1.7 billion text messages were sent in the USA during the third quarter of 2003, up from 1.2 billion in the first quarter.

At least some of the increase was down to new mobile phone service co-operatives that provide alibis for errant husbands and duplicitous wives. Today there are cell phone-based alibi clubs cropping up, which rapidly attract thousands of members ready to intervene on behalf of a stranger who feels unable to tell the truth to the spouse.

It works like this. Potential deceivers get in touch with one another through a dedicated Internet website. Then the person in need of an alibi sends out scores of text messages to the phones of collaborators. One will make contact and agree to make a plausible call to the escapee's home number while he is absent, backing up the lies he has already told.

If that wasn't enough to soothe a suspicious mind, then new background sound effects for cell phones might. At the touch of a button phones will be able to play the honking horns of a traffic jam, dentist drills or a symphony of roadworks – even when the user is prostrate on a beach somewhere.

The notion of an alibi club apparently evolved in Europe, and that's where one company has taken the business of lying one step further.

Love cheats in Germany can turn to the Perfect Alibi agency to help cover their tracks. For a nominal sum the firm will file an appropriate text message home at an agreed time. There are more costly dodges, though, including a fully-embossed seminar invitation complete with destination and telephone number tailored to fit that can be left lying on a mantelpiece at home while one partner gets up to whatever they choose. Perfect Alibi will then field telephone calls posing as a switchboard.

Company proprietor Jens Schlingensief believes he is providing a service necessary for modern life. I wonder if his wife would see it that way if he used such a service.

– JAILHOUSE ROCKS –

Britain's prison population stands at 74,700. In America the figure is almost 2.1 million.

Yet sometimes people prefer to be in prison than out, as two jailbirds proved after they absconded in darkness from Leyhill open prison in Gloucester, England. The pair walked through the early hours to Gloucester prison, administered by an altogether tougher regime, to turn themselves in. It wasn't that they sought freedom, but to live without the temptation of drugs which, they believed, were available to them inside Leyhill.

Audie Carr, 29, and Benjamin Clarke, 23, went walkabout after their requests for a prison transfer were denied. Both were charged with escape from lawful custody and spent time on remand in Gloucester jail. However, in June 2004 Judge Jamie Tabor QC, sitting at Gloucester Crown Court, agreed that it would not be in the public interest to prosecute the men, both of whom had conquered drug habits during a previous spell inside Gloucester prison, nor were they compelled to serve more time behind bars following the breakout. Clarke was serving an 18-month jail sentence for two offences of burglary and theft. Carr was serving a five-month sentence for assault.

At the same time prisoners from an Australian jail were apparently popping out at will but returning safe and sound before they were missed.

Problems began when a security system broke down at the Port Augusta prison. Although they were guarded by an officer, at least one prisoner was caught after slipping out to a party and buying some drugs. More prisoners might have been involved.

The boomerang effect is praiseworthy and, just to prove that not all prisoners are up to no good, a football team made up of inmates from Featherstone prison in Wolverhampton won a fair play award after going through a whole season without having a player sent off. The team was poised to win the league until six crucial players came to the end of their sentence and left the jail, causing the team to slip off the perch.

– WHAT'S IN A NAME? –

The most popular names chosen for babies in 2003 in the USA were Jacob (picked 29,195 times) and Emily (picked 25,494 times).

Thanks to the assiduous record-keeping carried out by the Social Security Administration in America we can compare the top ten names from last year to those most chosen between 1900 and 1909.

	Boy Names 2003	Boy Names 1900-09		Girl Names 2003	Girl Names 1900-09
1	Jacob	John	1	Emily	Mary
2	Michael	William	2	Emma	Helen
3	Joshua	James	3	Madison	Margaret
4	Matthew	George	4	Hannah	Anna
5	Andrew	Joseph	5	Olivia	Ruth
6	Joseph	Charles	6	Abigail	Elizabeth
7	Ethan	Robert	7	Alexis	Dorothy
8	Daniel	Frank	8	Ashley	Marie
9	Christopher	Edward	9	Elizabeth	Mildred
10	Anthony	Henry	10	Samantha	Alice

A parent might take more careful consideration of the naming process if he or she knew that girls called Katharine were found to have been the greatest GCSE UK exam achievers in 2003. Of the Katharines who sat exams that year, more than 88 per cent passed at least five. In descending order, the next most successful were Madeleines, Bryonys, Philippas and Eleanors.

But where there's a top of the table there's also a rear end, and this is occupied by the Dwaines in the class of 2003, of whom just 17 per cent scored more than five GCSEs. In ascending order the other ill-fated names were Wayne, Duane, Jermaine and Lance.

Many people dislike the name they were saddled with at birth, but few have greater cause than Saddam Hussein. Not Saddam Hussein the mad dictator presently under arrest in Iraq, but a much younger Iraqi fella, with a much better record on human rights. Despite being named for the notorious Iraqi president, Saddam the second has fled his country and is a Kurdish refugee in Norway.

'When my father chose the name 20 years ago, we didn't know what we now know about Saddam. The president was a respected man, even among Kurds. It wasn't shameful to be called "Saddam" then,' he explained.

Now he is seeking to change his name, not least to avoid the abusive telephone calls he has been getting from people who encounter his name in the telephone book. He isn't alone in having a name nightmare.

Steve Greenall always believed he possessed a regular, run-of-the-mill kind of name. So he was taken aback to see it writ large in a new advertisement for British Telecom. His surprise turned to horror when the name, featured on a mock-up of a business card, was followed by the words: 'Unreliable, Undependable, Unobtainable'.

You can't help but have some sympathy for Mr Greenall, an IT consultant, who feared the magazine advertisement put his reputation in peril.

However, the Advertising Standards Authority took a more relaxed view. The advertisement in question featured a ladder and a hammer and implied that Steve Greenall the second was a builder, so it rejected his complaint against the telecommunications giant. Afterwards, BT said it had picked on his name because it was uncommon but credible for advertising purposes.

According to scientists, parents should pay special attention to the words made by their offspring's initials if they want them to live a long life. A study by the University of San Diego of men's death certificates over 27 years proved that those with 'positive' word initials, like ACE and GOD, lived more than seven years longer than those who were a RAT, PIG or DUD.

– GIMME A V! –

Despite Winston Churchill's best efforts to transform it into a victory salute, the two-fingered V remains a swift, shocking symbol of contempt in the UK. It almost certainly stems from an era when English archers were causing havoc in France during the 14th and 15th centuries. If they were captured, the fingers necessary to operate the devastating long bows were frequently chopped off to keep them out of action. As a result, archers with digits intact would wave their two fingers at French opposition in defiance. It is a gesture largely unrecognised elsewhere in the world. Too bad UK pensioner Frank Benson doesn't live elsewhere. He waved two two-fingered salutes at a speed camera that flashed as he went past in Kendal, Cumbria, at a sedate and legal 32 kph (20 mph). The twin gestures were snapped on film and, having both hands off the steering wheel, he was charged in June 2004 with not being in control of his van.

The event happened three weeks after he had been fined £60 for driving at 70 kph in a 65 kph zone. This time South Lakeland magistrates fined him £100.

– READY FOR MY CLOSE-UP –

In the early 19th century, theatres did not have the benefit of electric lights. Nevertheless, the stage stars of the era sought illumination from limelights, flame-heated cylinders of lime placed next to a reflector to bounce off the glare. Actors competed for the best spot in the limelight and the phrase soon applied to anyone who looked for public attention.

– PILL POWER –

The five most popular anti-depressant drug brands in Britain – Prozac, Seroxat, Cipramil, Efexor and Lustral – together account for an average 49,000 prescriptions per day.

— ACKNOWLEDGEMENTS —

I'd like to thank my husband, Nick Constable, for his invaluable help in researching this book.

— ABOUT THE AUTHOR —

Karen Farrington is a journalist and the author of several books, including *Everything You Didn't Need to Know about the USA*, also publshed by Sanctuary. She lives in Exeter with her husband and three children.

— INDEX —